What people are saying about TANDEM

"Balancing the priorities of my marriage while meeting the demands of an international organization was not always easy. Unfortunately, back then, there wasn't a handbook on how to succeed in marriage and business at the same time. In their new book *Tandem*, Robert and Kay Lee neatly lay out many of the solutions to work-life balance that I had to learn the hard way. Whether you work together with your spouse or not, this is a must read."

HOWARD BEHAR
Retired President, Starbucks Corporation

"Entrepreneurship can be a great experience. The idea of creating something from scratch and building it into a thriving business is exhilarating. But there is a danger. We can get so focused on our work that we ignore our relationships with those we love. Robert and Kay Lee Fukui's new book, *Tandem*, has practical answers they have gleaned from their own entrepreneurial journey. Read this book and learn how to build a thriving and more profitable business while also building a great marriage. I highly recommend it."

CAROLYN CASTLEBERRY HUX
Speaker, author, and entrepreneur

"We know firsthand how entrepreneurial couples face their own unique set of challenges. Thankfully in their new book *Tandem*, Robert and Kay Lee Fukui give you a road map to face these challenges. Readers will find practical answers to help build a more profitable business while also building a strong relationship at home. We highly recommend it!"

KEVIN + STEPH MASON
Hosts of the nationally syndicated podcast *Tell Us a Good Story*

"Robert and Kay Lee Fukui know firsthand how difficult it is to build a great business while also building a strong marriage. They have been there and done that and now they have written a terrific book about it. For the entrepreneurs among us, *Tandem*: *The Married Entrepreneurs' Guide for Work-Life Balance*, will be a godsend. It's a handbook filled with practical and doable information. Pick up a copy. Keep it on your desk and refer to it often."

SARA CANADAY
Author, speaker, and entrepreneur

"*Tandem* is a must-read for every married couple, but especially those who want to work and love together in harmony! If you want your life, love and business to roll forward to the brightest future, we highly recommend reading *Tandem*, listening to Robert and Kay Lee's podcast (*Power Up Your Marriage and Business*) as their coaching is top-notch! We know this powerful, positive and proactive couple personally—they walk their talk—and make the work and marriage journey much more enjoyable!"

PAM AND BILL FARREL
Authors of 58 books including bestselling
Men Are Like Waffles, Women Are Like Spaghetti

"As a CEO and coach to those who have been in the C-Suite, I know firsthand how common it is for leaders and business owners to get addicted to 'the game' while ignoring those closest to them. It's an unhealthy and unsustainable way to live. I am honored to endorse this terrific book that offers a better way forward. *Tandem* authors Robert and Kay Lee Fukui are doing important work in this world. The people they serve and their families will be the beneficiaries."

JAY COUGHLAN
Co-Author of *Five Bold Choices* and CEO, Coughlan Consulting

"When it comes to striving for professional success, many couples feel they need to sacrifice quality time with family in order to accomplish that. Certainly, as a busy NFL football coach it is hard to win both on and off the field. But with intention, planning, and great teamwork as husband and wife, it is possible. Robert and Kay Lee do a beautiful job of laying out a game plan for business and marital success. I highly recommend *Tandem* for the married entrepreneur that is tired of sacrificing their family for business success and wants to start winning at both."

CLYDE CHRISTENSEN
NFL Quarterback Coach Tampa Bay Buccaneers

tandem

Laura,

You're wise beyond your years. Let your voice be heard!

ROBERT & KAY LEE FUKUI

tandem

THE MARRIED
ENTREPRENEURS' GUIDE
FOR GREATER WORK-LIFE BALANCE

tandem

The Married Entrepreneurs' Guide for Greater Work-Life Balance

ROBERT & KAY LEE FUKUI

Published by:
A Book's Mind
P.O. Box 272847
Fort Collins, CO 80527
ABooksMind.com

Cover design, interior layout and ebook by:
www.PearCreative.ca

Paperback ISBN: 978-1-953284-83-9

CONTENTS

ACKNOWLEDGMENTS

FROM ROBERT

This book is for all the entrepreneurs who are working to create a better life for themselves, their families, their employees, their vendors, their customers, and their communities. Family-run businesses are the backbone of our economy. Without you, there would be fewer opportunities.

It wasn't long ago when running my own business wasn't even a thought in my mind—let alone writing a book on the subject. So I want to thank my wife and business partner, Kay Lee, for believing I could do this before I even entertained the idea. Kay Lee, you have taught me that accepting the status quo relationship is not acceptable and that you *can* build a prosperous business while building a thriving marriage.

I want to thank my parents, Likio and Mildred, for their support, encouragement, and the belief that I can do anything I put my mind to. And for instilling in me the faith in God that brought me through some difficult times in my life.

To our editor, Libbye Morris, without whom we could not have completed this book. Thank you for being an encouragement and easy to work with.

Last but not least, thank you to our Heavenly Father. Without Him, none of this is possible.

FROM KAY LEE

To my dad—Even though being raised in a family business had many challenges, I am thankful for being raised in that environment because these businesses are the bread and butter of our community and economy. My dad taught me to have a good work ethic; to appreciate the freedoms of being my own boss; and that, with a dream and hard work, I can accomplish anything I put my mind to.

To my mom—The most enthusiastic encourager and cheerleader in my life. I get my family values and sense of adventure from her. She was the glue that kept the family together, holding down the fort inhabited by four strong-willed kids while my dad was running our business.

To my husband—One of the most committed persons I know, which is rare these days. He supports me, no matter what kind of crazy adventure I might come up with—well, at least most of them. He sees the best in people and can spot opportunities others do not notice. He always makes me look good and has my back.

Thank you to our Heavenly Father for guiding our every step along this path.

WHY WE WROTE THIS BOOK

Many times when Kay Lee and I are at the beach, she'll say excitedly, "Let's get on a tandem bike! It will be so fun."

My usual response is pretty lukewarm: "It doesn't seem like a good idea."

The way I see it, I can't have her in the front of the bike steering because she tends to get sidetracked. I worry that she would get so caught up in the beautiful scenery that she would steer us off path or run into a rollerblader. But if she is in the back, I'm not sure if she would be pedaling—for the same reasons. As I see it, in her mind, gazing at the crashing waves, pods of dolphins swimming off shore, or anything else that might catch her attention is more important than helping me power the bike.

Do you see the conundrum I face?

Put her in the front, and who knows where we will end up. Place her in the back, and we may get to our destination, but with more effort than I'd like to exert. Just because you and your spouse are riding together on a tandem bike frame, your bike seats welded together, doesn't mean you're going to be working together efficiently.

OK, I may be overdramatizing a bit, but this is how our Abbott and Costello routine goes.

What does this have to do with being married and owning a business?

Being successful in both marriage and business takes teamwork, whether or not you work for the same company. And teamwork starts with having a shared vision, knowing your respective roles, and communicating constantly.

If you've been married for even a minute, you know communication breakdowns happen on occasion. They also happen in business. Now put them together, and try to juggle both. In other words, marriage and business are each hard work on their own. But being married *and* running a business is a unique challenge that only 6.3 percent of the US population can relate to.[1]

That's right, you and I are in rarified air. We are among the weird ones who are willing to risk it all and sacrifice our time for the potential of greater freedom and higher earning potential.

A desire for freedom, satisfaction, and flexibility is actually the most common reason people start a business[2]—more so than trying to become the next Bill Gates. Of course, making a decent living is important, but

---

1 This figure is an extrapolation of two data points. The Kauffman Foundation found that 70 percent of entrepreneurs are married. (See "The Anatomy of an Entrepreneur," Ewing Marion Kauffman Foundation, July 8, 2009, https://www.kauffman.org/entrepreneurship/reports/the-anatomy-of-an-entrepreneur/#:~:text=The%20Anatomy%20of%20an%20Entrepreneur%20fills%20in%20some%20gaps%20by,the%20success%20of%20start%2Dups. Statista data from 2021 show that 8.9 percent of the US population owns a business. (See "Established Business Ownership Rate in North America in 2021, by Country," Statista, February 2022, https://www.statista.com/statistics/315556/established-business-ownership-rate-in-north-america.)

2 "The Top Reason Most Entrepreneurs Start Businesses," Shayna Waltower, *Business News Daily*, updated February 9, 2022. https://www.businessnewsdaily.com/4652-entrepreneur-motivation-benefits.html.

being able to set your own schedule and enjoy life to its fullest is the main priority for the average entrepreneur.

Your dream was to build a business so you could have more freedom. Has the dream become reality?

Having work–life balance—that is the dream, but unfortunately, the reality is much different. Business owners typically work more hours than if they were W-2 employees, take little time off, and cut their own pay before they cut their employees' pay. Instead of the owners running the business, the business runs them.

And the marriage? Oh boy. The stress of running a business compounds the stress of being married and raising a family. Husband and wife go into survival mode, acting like two ships passing in the night to keep things going.

If they had a vision, it's all lost in the daily grind of managing life. They may have started on a tandem bike, but they're acting as if they are riding separate unicycles.

We wrote this book because number one, we get it. Both of us were raised in households that reflected much of this dysfunction, and we noticed early on in our consulting practice that our clients were facing the same issue. After doing a bit of research on what the typical married entrepreneur deals with, it's clear that this lack of work–life balance and the separation it can create is all too common for the 6.3 percent of us.

You're not alone, and we want to help.

We want to help you and your spouse get on the same page, create healthy boundaries between work and home, and structure your business so it can prosper while giving you back the time you want and the freedom you deserve.

Balancing business and marriage—and being successful at both—is possible. Are you ready?

Entrepreneurs are typically so busy building their businesses that they end up sacrificing the quality of their marriage and personal life. They struggle to achieve work–life balance. This book explains how to regain that balance, prioritize your marriage, work well as a team, and create a more efficient business. Each chapter contains the following:

1. A relevant story about our own journey and/or a story about entrepreneurs we have worked with
2. Reflection questions to guide you in applying the strategies in this book to your own situation
3. A QR code to use in downloading a digital workbook for you and your spouse to study together as you apply the strategies we recommend to your life and business

Plenty of books offer advice on how to *have a strong marriage* or how to *manage a successful business*. But there aren't many books on how to do both well—at the same time. We wrote *Tandem* to help married entrepreneurs end the all-too-common power struggles that arise when trying to build a thriving marriage while also growing a business—whether or not they work in the same business.

Let's get started! In chapter 1, we set the stage for the strategies in this book by sharing a bit of our journey with you.

Chapter 1
HOW WE GOT HERE

Merge all your yesterdays into a brilliant tomorrow.

"Experience is a lesson of the past to lessen the burden of the future." | Michael Sage

They say communication is the key to a successful relationship. Well, I certainly got a good taste of what that was going to be like with my wife, Kay Lee, on our very first date.

We met on an online dating site in 2004. After trading emails for about a week, we had our first chat on the phone. A week after that, we scheduled our first date. Because Kay Lee lived an hour from my home in Pasadena, California, I arranged to drive out to her location in Ventura, California, to meet. And because she was only ten minutes from the beach, it made a good excuse to arrange a sunset dinner at a nice seafood restaurant on the pier.

I waited outside the restaurant for her to arrive. When she walked up the stairs, I immediately noticed she was even better looking in person than in her online photos. Don't get me wrong—her photos were good, but sometimes, you never know. So this was a bonus!

We enjoyed a lovely sunset dinner and got to know each other better in person. She was just as personable face-to-face as she was on the phone.

After dinner, we took a little stroll along the pier. As I walked her to her car, I told her, "I had a really good time."

She said, "So did I."

I asked her, "Do you want to do this again?"

She shrugged her shoulders and said, "Eh, OK."

This unenthusiastic response was not what I was looking for.

While I was surprised at her response, and a little disappointed, I thought, "Well, at least she didn't say no."

I was trying to figure out if Kay Lee's response meant she wasn't really into me. But she *said* she had a good time. I was relying on my years of marketing and sales training to better understand her intent, so I asked a follow-up question: "I'll be back in town on Wednesday. Do you want to go out for dinner again?"

She hesitated but finally said OK.

Whew! Got that figured out. It was better to get a solid yes or no answer now than drive an hour home wondering if I should call her again. Granted, we had just met. But it was obvious to us both that if this was going to go anywhere, we would need to communicate more effectively.

This is an example of how a lack of effective communication can be the source of much frustration for most couples. When a message from our spouse isn't clear, we tend to make assumptions about what he or she means, instead of just asking for clarification. This can cause a lot of unnecessary conflict. Many studies show that up to 80 percent of our interpretation of what someone says is based on *how* it was said, not on the words spoken. In the absence of facts, we tend to fill in the gaps with what we *believe* is true.

I feel like I have always been a good listener. But even good listening skills cannot guarantee clear communication with your spouse. Whether you know someone well or not, asking clarifying questions is the key to preventing conflict and having good communication. To this day, Kay Lee and I can still find ourselves misunderstanding each other because we don't clarify what we think the other means.

A lot of people would have given up on that relationship, given Kay Lee's apparent lack of interest. Her body language and nonverbal communication were telling me, "She's not into me." But she *said* she had a good time and that she wanted to go out again. So instead of assuming the worst, I took her at her word and asked her out for a second date. Sometimes, ignorance is bliss.

My (Kay Lee's) thought was that I didn't want to seem too eager. I know that most men like a challenge—a "chase." Also, my family doesn't like to commit. So I figured a noncommittal answer would let me off the hook, and he wouldn't pursue me any further. He would think I wasn't interested, and I would just move on.

**Never assume you understand what someone means.
Ask questions to clarify.**

As you can see, understanding how to communicate well with Kay Lee wasn't just about asking clarifying questions; it was important for me to know her noncommittal personality style as well. This would prove to be a challenge over time.

KAY LEE'S EARLY BUSINESS BACKGROUND: A LACK OF WORK-LIFE BALANCE AFFECTS THE CHILDREN, TOO

I (Kay Lee) am a third-generation entrepreneur. My grandpa was a real estate investor and painting contractor, and my dad ran a feed store. So I grew up in a small-family-business environment.

It was a big struggle for our family to balance work and family time. My dad worked six days a week, so we didn't see him much. It was hard on my mom, and it was hard on us as a family. It was stressful for us. We just wanted to have our dad around more often and have more family time. I think it was stressful for him, too, because he was the family's breadwinner.

My Dad's Business Was the Mistress

It almost seemed like my dad's business was the mistress because it took all his time, and we were competing with the business. In our consulting work today, Robert and I find this to be a common phenomenon among couples in business: one or both people work so much that the job actually competes with the marriage.

In spite of my dad's crazy schedule, our family did manage to go on one family vacation each year. I was thankful for that alone time with Dad, away from his business. It made me wish it could happen more often.

Then, when I turned thirteen, my dad told me, "You're going to work." So I started working in his business.

I was shy and quiet, and my dad just threw me out there. Before long, I was spending all my time at the feed store on the weekends and after school on weekdays. Learning to greet the clients and give them great customer service was a challenge for me. It was difficult for me to have conversations with people and look them in the eye. It was hard work but a great learning experience.

And that is exactly what my dad expected—hard work. He, too, grew up with a very strong work ethic and high expectations. His parents owned a dairy, so he worked a lot of hours, beginning when he was a child. I think he wanted me to develop the same work ethic his dad had instilled in him at a young age. It got to the point where he could really rely on me and not have to be around the business as much.

I am the oldest of four children; I have two sisters and a brother. But for some reason, my dad didn't require them to work in the business. By the time they got to be thirteen or so, he had already come to rely on me a lot. One of my sisters took my place for a while, but I ended up going back.

My mom didn't work in the business much. She was busy raising four strong-willed kids and keeping the household running. With Dad working day and night and Mom taking care of the family, they were like two ships passing in the night. Needless to say, they didn't have a strong marriage. Having a strong work ethic is a great characteristic, but it can create conflict if overdone.

I am sure this experience has shaped my views on how a business can become a detriment to a marriage and family if not managed well.

HOW BUSINESS ISSUES AFFECT THE CHILDREN

In my younger years, I (Kay Lee) was glad to spend time working closely with my dad. Because he was usually at work, the best way to spend time with him was to work with him. It also taught me some great life skills because I had to interact with customers, vendors, do a little sales, and handle basic bookkeeping. Plus, I got paid! Not a lot of kids my age were working, and those who worked for their family business weren't getting paid.

This allowed me to purchase my first car—a Camaro! That was cool.

But working in a family business was not always easy. Like many family businesses, work was all-consuming, and taking time off was a challenge. The feed store my dad owned was open Monday through Saturday, and while we had a small staff, the major responsibilities fell on my dad and then me. No one else in the family worked in the business.

That meant if there was a family event or outing, my dad and I couldn't both take time off at the same time. As you might guess, I usually drew the short straw. I couldn't attend my own sister's college graduation because my dad went, and I had to run the store.

My dad would tell me once in a while that I was going to take over the store someday. However, that was where the conversation would end. Deep down, I knew I didn't want to take it over because it didn't hold the best of memories.

This is a common scenario—the business owner plans for the kids to take it over, but because of negative experiences, the kids usually have other ideas. Many times, the business doesn't get passed on to the kids because of the lifestyle issue, not a financial one.

So the lack of work–life balance not only disrupts the relationship between husband and wife; it can damage the bond between parents and children as well.

How does your business affect your children? Check in with them to find out how they are feeling about things. Encourage them to share their ideas and concerns.

MY EARLY EXPERIENCES AS A PASTOR'S KID

Although I (Robert) didn't have an entrepreneurial background like Kay Lee did, my dad was a pastor. There are many similarities between running a small business and running a ministry.

I was born in Hawaii, and my dad pastored several churches on several of the islands when I was growing up. He had a lot to take care of as a pastor, and the members of his congregation were a lot like customers in a business.

Family Businesses and Ministries Share Some Dynamics

Like a lot of people in ministry—and in business—my dad poured his heart and soul into his role as a pastor. Like Kay Lee, I felt like our dad put the family on the "back burner" because he was so busy taking care of the flock. This is a common dynamic in ministries. I hear about it more and more now. We have talked with a lot of people whose families are involved in building ministries, and they say they also experience a lack of work–life balance.

My mother was a stay-at-home mom, just as Kay Lee's mom was. She helped the church a lot behind the scenes, but she was mostly at home, raising my older sister and me.

When I got into college, I knew I did not want to become a pastor. So I majored in business. Soon after selecting business as a major, I fell in love with marketing and decided to concentrate in this area. Before Kay Lee and I started our consulting business, I spent my entire career with Fortune 500 companies, working in marketing and sales.

Even though I'm an introvert at heart, I enjoyed a very successful career in marketing and sales. I won a number of sales and leadership awards, won amazing international trips, helped launch six global brands, and was personally responsible for more than $150 million in sales.

Around 2013, I started trying to figure out what my next step would be—what did I want to do for the rest of my life? I was in my early forties, and I knew I wanted to do something different from the corporate path.

When Kay Lee and I were dating, she would say, "I can see you having a business." But that vision didn't come naturally to me like it did to her because that's not how I grew up. My dad always told me, "Go to college, get good grades, stay out of debt, and get a good career." So that's what I did. I never really thought about having a business.

My First Experience with Work-Life Imbalance

With Kay Lee encouraging me, I contemplated what kind of business I would start. She had always seen me as an entrepreneur, but I didn't see that path for myself at first.

Try as I might, I couldn't come up with anything. I even printed out a list of the North American Industry Classification System (NAICS, pronounced "nakes") codes and all the different types of businesses. I crossed out each one—nope, nope, nope. Finally, I decided that because I have a background, education, and experience in marketing, I would do marketing consulting for a while. I was looking at it as paid market research—getting paid by various companies to improve their marketing while also getting to learn a variety of businesses. I figured that if I did that long enough, eventually I would find something I liked.

As it turns out, I really enjoyed consulting, so I decided it would be my next step outside the corporate world—at least until I found a more traditional type of business to start.

When starting out, I consulted mostly owners of small and medium-sized businesses—primarily family-owned businesses. Pretty quickly, I noticed a commonality among these business owners—they were working much harder than they needed to. Although they were calling me for my marketing expertise, their biggest issues did not center around marketing. Instead, a big part of the problem was that many of these entrepreneurs were unaware of sound business fundamentals.

This is what was creating a work–life imbalance. Because the businesses did not have solid business fundamentals in place, there were many inefficiencies. To make up for that, the owner and staff would work harder. And as we shared about our childhood experiences, working harder means less time with the spouse and family.

What Kay Lee and I typically see is that small-business owners are good at a craft, so they start charging money for it and making a living out of it. They basically learn how to run the businesses as they go. The learn-as-you-go method can work to some extent, but eventually, it leads to a lot of gaps in the management of these companies. This is why many small-business owners end up spending a lot more time in the business than they should. Instead of working smarter, they're working harder.

In 2016, I left the corporate environment and began consulting on a full-time basis. But before I left the corporate world and officially launched our business, Kay Lee helped me get ready. Once I was a full-time consultant, she would take trips with me and meet our clients. Some of the couples we met with owned businesses together, while others either stayed home and raised the family or had their own business or career.

As we coached small-business owners in marketing and other operational areas to improve the bottom line of the business, we noticed a pervasive dynamic that characterized most of these working couples—a power struggle between the marriage and the business. Just as we shared in our respective stories about the way we grew up, these businesses took center stage in the owners' lives and created a work–life imbalance.

This struggle creates a lot of conflict, which most couples are not skilled in resolving. As a result, many marriages and/or businesses end up failing. We learned that with some guidance and by putting the right strategies in place for the marriage and business, business owners succeed at both.

Entrepreneurs' lives get out of balance when they react to what life gives them instead of planning how they want to live life.

Though at first, our business was focused primarily on improving business performance, people inevitably would talk with us about their personal lives and marriages. We found ourselves naturally coaching them on how to improve communication and navigate conflict. We believe it doesn't matter what the nature of the conflict is—if you can discuss it and resolve it successfully, you have a chance for success, harmony, and marriage–work balance.

"Marriage" Counseling—On Our Fourth Date!

Kay Lee and I got past our initial challenges to figure out if we should move forward, and we had four great dates. After our interesting first date, we had our second, third, and fourth dates. It was at this point that she laid another bomb on me—she suggested I see a therapist.

Were we even an item? You know, dating exclusively. She went from acting like she wasn't interested in a second date to suggesting I see a therapist, as though we were an old couple already.

I (Kay Lee) believed I had a good reason for suggesting counseling for Robert before our relationship progressed. Here's why.

Robert was previously married—to his grade-school sweetheart. He loved her very much. Unfortunately, one day, right before Christmas, she was driving to work on the 110 freeway, and she got into a horrific car accident and was killed instantly. Of course it was devastating for him, and he grieved about the loss a lot.

He would have still been with her if she had not passed away. I just wanted to make sure I was not getting into a relationship that might have difficulty moving forward because of the sense of loss he felt. Robert has a huge heart, but I wanted to make sure that he had room for me in his heart—and his life. I did not want to feel like I was competing with a ghost"—his first relationship. And I wanted to find that out sooner, not later.

It would have been devastating for me if I were to put my whole heart into it and then find out he didn't have room for me in his life.

Navigating Grief and Moving Forward

I (Robert) understood Kay Lee's concern.

Unfortunately, the way I had learned to grieve was by supporting my first wife through the death of her mother and father. Her mother had passed away two and half years before she did. Then, two years later, her father passed away. By that time, I had learned valuable lessons about grieving after the passing of my wife. By the time I met Kay Lee, I felt I had grieved properly and therefore didn't think I needed counseling.

Yet I didn't want my resistance to seeing a therapist prevent my relationship with Kay Lee from going forward. So I found a counselor in my network and scheduled an appointment. It turned out that she was helpful in guiding me as I continued to process my grief. After just one session, the counselor felt I had grieved in a heathy way and told me she thought I was ready to move forward with my life.

When I saw Kay Lee next, she asked me, "How'd it go?"

I said, "She gave me the thumbs up, the seal of approval. She thinks I'm OK to be in a relationship with you."

That was not the end of it, as I expected, because Kay Lee didn't buy my therapist's assessment. She said, "You should go see *my* counselor."

"Seriously?" I thought. "What is it going to take to please this woman?"

Because Ventura was in my sales territory, I worked out my schedule so I could end my day there and meet with her counselor. Afterward, I would go pick Kay Lee up for dinner. She always wanted to know the details about my counseling sessions. I was like a lot of men—I didn't really feel comfortable discussing the details. Plus, I had just spent an hour talking about these issues, and I didn't want to relive the whole hour again.

So I suggested that Kay Lee just go with me to see the counselor. That way, she could ask follow-up questions while we were there, and we wouldn't have to have the back-and-forth discussions again. At first, she said, "No. These are your sessions." But then she agreed to go with me. After the first few session, our time with the therapist turned from focusing on my grief to plain old relationship counseling. That continued for two years, until the day we got married.

During those two years, Kay Lee and I learned how to communicate and to resolve conflict, among other valuable skills that are critical in both personal and professional relationships. Honestly, I was not for counseling, but if it hadn't been for those sessions, our first years of marriage would have been difficult. And might still be difficult.

Just like the average business owner is not trained to run a business, the average person is not trained to manage conflict and communicate well. So getting professional help on both ends will increase your chances of success with marriage and business.

Research shows, and our experience confirms, it's easier to fix and strengthen a relationship when things are going pretty well than it is when the couple's relationship is on its last leg. Too many times, couples turn to counseling as a last resort.

We also saw the benefit of going together and having a third party be the coach as we walked through various challenges in our relationship. That's why we prefer working with a married entrepreneur and the spouse at the same time. Sure, coaching one of the spouses can help, but we see greater progress faster when working with them together.

UNHEALTHY MARRIAGES AFFECT BUSINESSES, AND VICE VERSA

As you can see, we've had real-world experience in being on the receiving end of poor work–life balance as we were growing up. While neither one of us had healthy communication or conflict resolution modeled to us, we were fortunate to have professional guidance to do that better in our marriage.

So we understand how a lack of work–life balance can affect a marriage. You start this business because you want more freedom and unlimited earning potential. But instead, it keeps you in more bondage to work than if you had a regular W-2 position.

When you're married, there will naturally be some conflict that arises from various life decisions that need to be made. But when you're also faced with the additional demands of running a business, it only intensifies the problems.

As we started consulting and heard the professional and personal power struggles our clients were facing, we knew we had to address them head-on.

There are *marriage* counselors and coaches. And there are *business* consultants and coaches. But neither addresses both sides of the issue. So if married entrepreneurs were to get marriage help while their businesses were still struggling, they would still be faced with some significant challenges. And vice versa.

This is why we've been on this journey over the past several years to pass along the communication and conflict-resolution tools that will help any marital situation while also sharing best business practices that will help you work smarter, not harder. The strategies we share in this book will position your business to scale and grow while giving you time back to invest into the relationships that matter most—those your spouse and family.

Our lives get out of balance because we've allowed it to happen. Sure, things happen that are beyond our control, but for the most part, we have more control of our lives than not.

It's not easy, but with intention, you can create better balance in your marriage and business. You can have a thriving marriage *and* a prosperous business!

YOU DO NOT HAVE TO FIGURE THIS OUT ON YOUR OWN

We love that we get to help married entrepreneurs like you. Our clients have told us the skills they are learning are "a breath of fresh air." Finally, they have solutions to issues they thought were just a fact of life. Like our parents before us, entrepreneurs have accepted a "truth" that you can't have both a thriving marriage and a prosperous business—that you will have to sacrifice your personal life if you wish to succeed in business. They are extremely relieved to discover that their marriages and their businesses can thrive when they take some basic steps to manage the dynamics surrounding both.

Our clients also tell us they are relieved to discover that they don't have to navigate these challenges alone. Owning a business can be very isolating. Often, business owners keep issues to themselves because they don't want to burden their spouses or families. But that does not help solve the issues. Kay Lee and I dive in, head-first, to help couples like you discover—and heal—the issues that prevent you from having the best possible marriage and the most successful business possible.

In chapter 2, we discuss strategies for achieving a healthier balance between your marriage and your business.

TANDEM BIKE CHECK

Scan the QR code below, or visit thetandembook.com/chapter-1, to watch a short video of us discussing this chapter. Also, you can download a free digital workbook that will help you create better balance in business and marriage.

Chapter 2
BALANCE MARRIAGE AND BUSINESS

Keep the priorities the priority.

"The key is not to prioritize what's on your schedule but to schedule your priorities." | Stephen Covey

Work–life balance, which is really the same as marriage–business balance, is the unicorn many entrepreneur couples are chasing, but many give up before they find it. Most of us have just accepted the fact that we can excel either in business or in marriage, but not in both. That is fake news! Achieving greater balance in your marriage and business is possible; it simply requires that you and your spouse take action together, in tandem. It takes intention, planning, creating boundaries, preparation, and letting go of control.

People start their own businesses for a variety of reasons—often to gain more autonomy, flexibility, and work–life balance than their corporate jobs provide. Yet those ideals can seem like a distant, disappearing mirage once the business is up and running.

A 2020 study from Cox Business found that more than half of small business owners start their own business so they can *be their own boss.* The researchers found that entrepreneurs were also motivated by the idea of *creating something from the ground up*. Almost two-thirds of respondents in the survey said they had started their own business for one of those reasons. Money wasn't a big motivation—just 8 percent of small-business owners said money was their main motivation for starting a business.[3]

But sadly, once they launch their businesses, many entrepreneurs end up with even *less* work–life balance than they had before. They put so much time, effort, and money into trying to launch and grow their businesses that their marriage and family life—and even their health—can suffer. Suddenly, that dream of freedom turns into a nightmare of bondage!

Why did you start your own business?
To what extent have you achieved your original vision of autonomy, flexibility, and work–life balance?

3 "The No. 1 Reason Most Entrepreneurs Start Businesses," *Business News Daily*, updated February 20, 2020, https://www.businessnewsdaily.com/4652-entrepreneur-motivation-benefits.html.

SMALL BUSINESSES ARE THE BACKBONE OF THE US ECONOMY

We are passionate about helping the married entrepreneur thrive at home and work because we've witnessed the struggles firsthand, from childhood to present. Also, small businesses drive our nation's economy, so the work we do is important, both financially and relationally.

Almost all—99.9 percent—of the businesses in the United States are small businesses, defined as those with fewer than five hundred employees, according to 2019 US Small Business Administration statistics.

We are committed to helping American businesses succeed. Many of them need guidance in various aspects of business operation, from market analysis to increasing efficiency in operations to managing cash flow. Most entrepreneurs start their businesses because they're good at what they do and can charge money for that service. However, few entrepreneurs have formal business training; they tend to learn as they go. The result is that they often struggle to become and stay profitable, the owners work too hard, and financial problems can get out of control before anyone knows there's a problem.

According to the Small Business Administration, 20 percent of small businesses fail in the first year, 50 percent fail after five years, and only 33 percent stay in business for ten years or longer.[4] Some of the most common reasons small businesses fail are that they run out of money;

4 "The 4 Most Common Reasons a Small Business Fails," Melissa Horton, Investopedia, updated March 31, 2022, https://www.investopedia.com/articles/personal-finance/120815/4-most-common-reasons-small-business-fails.asp

the owners lack experience in managing a business or are unwilling to delegate routine tasks to others; there is no business plan; and the marketing campaigns are poorly planned or executed. These are among the issues that drag down small businesses.

Just as most entrepreneurs lack formal business training, most couples have not gone through formal marriage counseling. The Gottman Institute in Seattle, founded by Dr. John Gottman and his wife, Dr. Julie Schwartz Gottman, have conducted decades of research on the topic of marital success. They say only 31 percent of married couples engage in counseling before marriage, and only 19 percent seek counseling during marriage. Also, the average couple waits six years before seeking professional help for marital problems.[5]

So it's no wonder that couples struggle on both sides—in business and in marriage. We address the dynamics of both sides of the equation as we work with couples. A first step is to define what marriage–work balance looks like for you and your spouse. You can't achieve what you don't define. This is different for every couple, based on their circumstances, business model, family situations, upbringing, and other factors.

THE INTENDED SOLUTION OFTEN BECOMES A NEW PROBLEM

The startup businesses that entrepreneurs launch in an effort to solve their work–life balance issues often end up creating more problems. New business owners often end up spending every waking moment marketing their services, establishing their clientele, and completing

5 "Is it Time to Go to Couples Counseling?" Kyle Benson, The Gottman Institute, https://www.gottman.com/blog/is-it-time-to-go-to-couples-counseling/

client work. Many people sacrifice their marriages and families for the sake of their businesses, reasoning, "This is what it takes to be successful."

When entrepreneurs decide to focus primarily on their business, they can be asking for trouble at home. Here's why. The spouse wants time, attention, and connection, but instead, he or she gets the leftovers. Even when the entrepreneur is home and may be eating dinner with the family, he or she is exhausted and distracted—not really present.

Here's the struggle that goes on in entrepreneurs' minds: "If I make more money, I'll have more time. But I need to spend more time to make more money." It's a mad cycle. They discover that they have lost control and now life is happening to them. Business becomes the *de facto* priority. The ends justify the means.

If you prioritize your marriage, you can still make a lot of money. But if you prioritize money, your marriage will suffer.

As couples' work–marriage imbalance gets worse, the finger-pointing begins. Spouses often start blaming each other for the imbalance.

Good news! This is fixable. A first step in correcting the imbalance is for both spouses to recognize that they are both part of the problem—and part of the solution. Both parties have played a part in aggravating the situation. And both can work to resolve the problem.

When the underlying issues of imbalance are not addressed, marriages often end in divorce—or, at the very least, couples' intimacy erodes, and they end up living like mere roommates. Statistics on the divorce rate for entrepreneur couples are difficult to find because no data are tracked on this issue. Yet many divorce attorneys say the divorce rate for entrepreneur couples is higher (some estimate as much as 10 percent higher) than it is for the general population.

Earlier, we mentioned the research on marriages conducted by the Gottman Institute in Seattle. Dr. John Gottman and his wife, Dr. Julie Schwartz Gottman, cofounded the organization and have conducted decades of research on the topic.

In 2019, as the Jeff and McKenzie Bezos divorce shocked the world, Dr. Julie Gottman wrote, "What happens typically, if the man is more the predominant entrepreneur, is that he devotes himself completely to the business, working as much as 18 to 20 hours a day, seven days a week, and the partner or wife is often the one who is raising the children and later on taking on perhaps some responsibilities for charity work or foundational work. What ends up happening is they end up diverging in terms of their world. They're really living in two separate worlds."[6]

Clearly, that all-too-familiar scenario is the opposite of marriage–work balance. Before Kay Lee and I can even begin to work on our clients' marketing, networking, or digital-automation strategies, we must identify and resolve issues related to this all-consuming imbalance between the marriage and the business.

How strong is your marriage–work balance?
To find out, take our free seven-question survey:
www.powercouplesbydesign.com/your-power-couple-score

6 "Bezos Divorce Highlights Hidden Challenge for Company Founders: Keeping Their Marriages Intact," Kurt Schlosser, GeekWire, January 11, 2019, https://www.geekwire.com/2019/bezos-divorce-highlights-hidden-challenge-company-founders-keeping-marriages-intact/

WORKING TOO MUCH CAN LEAD TO HEALTH ISSUES

Not only does working too many hours damage our relationships and our quality of life; it can damage our health, too.

According to a 2021 World Health Organization study, people who work 55 or more hours each week face an estimated 35 percent higher risk of a stroke and a 17 percent higher risk of dying from heart disease, compared to people following the widely accepted standard of working 35 to 40 hours in a week. The WHO study notes that when teleworking became the norm in many industries during the COVID-19 pandemic, boundaries were blurred between home and work. Also, many businesses were forced to either scale back or shut down their operations to save money, and the people who remained on the payroll ended up working longer hours.[7]

Kay Lee and I are all too familiar with this reality. The good news is, our personal experience with this struggle to gain balance means we understand your struggles, and we can help you achieve more balance between your work life and your marriage.

How many hours per week do you work now?
How many hours per week would you like to work?

7 "Overwork Killed More Than 745,000 People in a Year, WHO Study Finds," Bill Chappell, National Public Radio, May 17, 2021, https://www.npr.org/2021/05/17/997462169/thousands-of-people-are-dying-from-working-long-hours-a-new-who-study-finds

MORE ABOUT OUR STORY: FROM SIDE HUSTLE TO FULL-TIME BUSINESS

You already know part of our story. But here is more background about how our own work–marriage imbalance arose.

In 2014, when I was developing my marketing-consulting business, with the hope of leaving my corporate job in pharmaceuticals, my punishing work schedule was manageable. But as time went on and the business began to grow, it got tougher. Then it got to the point where I was exhausted on the weekends. I just wanted to rest. In fact, as soon as I woke up in the morning, I wanted to take a nap right away! I tried to reserve the weekends for personal time for Kay Lee and me. But because I was so mentally and physically exhausted, I wasn't very "present," mentally or emotionally.

Kay Lee was OK with the situation at first because in her mind, it was temporary. I thought it would be temporary, too. I figured that once I quit my corporate job and began consulting on a full-time basis, I would get my life back, and Kay Lee would get her husband back. I was conscious about making sure that when I left the full-time job, I didn't backfill my newly found time in the evenings with other activities that would consume all my focus and energy. But still, I ended up working more hours, and harder, than I had intended when I launched my consulting business.

WE EXPERIENCED THE SAME MARRIAGE–WORK BALANCE ISSUES OUR CLIENTS HAVE

As we began to coach and consult small-business owners, we saw that they were having the exact same challenges that we were experiencing!

There was a significant imbalance between the amount of time and energy we spent on work and on our marriages.

In trying to build and grow our businesses to provide for our families, we all were giving our marriages the short end of the stick. Our lack of work–life balance affected our businesses and our personal lives negatively.

Again, even though our consulting business started out with a focus on marketing, we realized that before we could even get to discussions about marketing, we needed to help them correct their marriage–work imbalance. We saw how hard they were working on the imbalance it caused in their lives. It became our motivation to help them in all aspects of their business so they could build more profitable businesses while getting their lives back.

When we began consulting married entrepreneurs, we noticed that most of them had a lot of inefficiencies in their businesses. They worked way too hard. We began helping them see those issues and resolve them so they could get their personal lives—and their healthy marriages—back. Meanwhile, Kay Lee and I were struggling with the same issues. So we tried to take our own advice and do something differently.

WE SET PRIORITIES TO WORK ON THE BUSINESS MORE

We sat down and wrote out our priorities, just like we ask our clients to do. We listed the activities we needed to work on most to *grow* the consulting business, and we listed daily business activities we could delegate or stop doing altogether. We wanted to work less and spend more time together, get to bed at a decent time, and enjoy the evenings and weekends instead of being wiped out.

Our goal—both for us and for our clients—was to free up some time so we could work *on* our business more and work *in* our business less. We will discuss this concept more in chapter 8, "Increase Your Time Margin."

According to The Alternative Board (TAB), a few years ago, entrepreneurs spent an average of 68.1 percent of their time working "in" their businesses—tackling day-to-day tasks, putting out fires, etc.—and only 31.9 percent of their time working "on" their business, such as long-term goals and strategic planning. The TAB survey also showed that most business owners (63 percent) were working more than 50 hours a week, but the average entrepreneur wanted to work 41.7 hours. The study revealed that ineffective time management was the root cause of entrepreneurs working too much.[8]

When you spend more time on long-term-growth activities such as research and development, pursuing high-value clients, training your team, and improving systems and technology, business growth happens.

This is an area that many business owners like us fail to spend enough time on, and it is the primary reason companies get stuck. So the first thing we do for our clients is determine how much time they are spending on various activities. Then we help them discover which activities they need to spend less time on—maybe by using specific types of software or hiring an assistant. We also help them identify things they should say "no" to, for now or forever.

As entrepreneurs, we need to spend our time on client work and growth-oriented activities and less time on putting out fires, routine

8 "Time Management: New Survey Reveals How Biz Owners Are Spending Their Time—And How They'd Rather Spend It," Richard Carufel, Agility PR Solutions, February 26, 2016, https://www.agilitypr.com/pr-news/business/time-management-new-survey-reveals-biz-owners-spending-time-theyd-rather-spend.

administrative activities, and daily personnel matters. Read on to discover one of the strategies Kay Lee and I share with our clients to work smarter instead of harder.

What percent of your time do you spend working *in* your business, and what percent do you spend working *on* your business? The ideal ratio is to spend 70 percent of your time *on* the business and 30 percent of your time *in* the business. What steps can you take to free up your time so you can work more *on* the business?

Every *couple* faces challenges, such as communicating well, resolving conflict, and prioritizing quality time together. Every *business owner* faces challenges as well, such as making the business profitable, working smarter instead of harder, and balancing time spent on the business and with family. The business owner is the person who will ultimately take the lead on employing strategies to operate the business more efficiently.

Too often, those challenges go unaddressed. The result is that couples either sacrifice the marriage for the business, or they sacrifice the business for the marriage. As neutral and experienced consultants/coaches who specialize in this unique challenge, we can see your situation from a new perspective. Our outside observations can make a significant difference in your ability to solve power struggles and achieve marriage–work balance. Many times, couples cannot see the source of their issues. And if they can't figure it out on their own, they tend to keep interacting with the same unhealthy patterns.

We hope this book helps you identify and understand obstacles to marriage–work balance and to discover solutions that can help you and your partner move past them. We specialize in leading our clients to build a business, build a marriage, and succeed at both.

DON'T BELIEVE THE BIG LIE!

Many entrepreneurs have bought into the lie that they have to sacrifice their personal lives to succeed in business. They believe their businesses will thrive more if they put more time into them. The more they focus on the business, the more the quality of their marriage and family life suffers. The business gets their best, while the spouse and family get the sloppy seconds or thirds. Yet all this time they're spending at work isn't increasing their profitability, efficiency, or success. Meanwhile, their health, relationships, and personal life begins to erode. Please don't buy into this myth!

Putting in more time in your business is not the answer. Making more sales is not the answer, either. The solution is, instead, to work smarter instead of harder. By implementing the practical strategies we offer in this book, you will begin to run your business more efficiently. This will enable you to spend quality time with your spouse and family and quality time in your business.

It is possible to prioritize your spouse, family, and personal life while building a highly successful business. But it takes some intentional planning and the willingness to approach things a bit differently. Our goal is to share strategies with you that have guided our clients to highly improved work–life balance. We want you to enjoy all aspects of your life while building a thriving business.

AVOID THE REGRETS MANY ENTREPRENEURS HAVE

The "hustle" of entrepreneurship is often glorified. Many business owners wear their 24/7 work schedule as a badge of honor, when, in reality, they're just burning themselves out. Some entrepreneurs never realize how much their lack of work–life balance is affecting them. Others realize it when it's too late—ill health forces them to retire or they reach retirement age, broken, divorced, and full of regrets.

Alexa Von Tobel, founder and CEO of LearnVest, mentions one of the most common regrets among hard-charging entrepreneurs. "I should have slept a bit more and tried to take care of myself a bit better," she writes. "I really was grinding myself to the bone." Funlayo Alabi, CEO and cofounder of Shea Radiance, says she wishes she'd had a more realistic idea of how long it would take to achieve the growth she wanted. "Pace yourself," Alabi advises. "This is a marathon, not a sprint, so conserve your energy!"[9]

Additional regrets entrepreneurs often have are wishing they had nurtured their inner circle more, wishing they hadn't worked so hard, and wishing they had made themselves happier.[10] Jason DeMers, a productivity expert and the CEO of EmailAnalytics, notes two more common regrets among entrepreneurs: not taking enough personal

9 "5 Entrepreneurs Reveal Their Biggest Mistakes (So You Can Avoid Making Them, Too)," US Chamber of Commerce, February 25, 2019, https://www.uschamber.com/co/start/strategy/entrepreneurs-biggest-regrets

10 "Top 6 Regrets of a Dying Entrepreneur," SuccessStory.com, date unknown, https://successstory.com/inspiration/regrets-of-a-dying-entrepreneur

time and not hiring the right people.[11] And finally, Karl Pillemer, a gerontologist at Cornell University, is the author of *30 Lessons for Living: Tried and True Advice from the Wisest Americans.* His team interviewed 1,500 people over the age of sixty-five to find out what haunted them most about their life choices. Among the top eight regrets of these older Americans were not resolving a family estrangement, putting off saying how they feel, and not traveling enough.[12]

The best way to avoid regrets is to take a close, honest look at your life today, identify areas where you're struggling, and then take steps to make improvements. Often, this requires that you let go of some control and ask for some help—two major themes in this book.

CHALLENGES BUSINESSES FACE

As you will discover in this book, the epidemic lack of work–life balance among married entrepreneurs is largely rooted in a lack of understanding about, and tracking of, financial metrics and key performance indicators. Most entrepreneurs have little or no formal education or training in financial management. One consequence is that the average profit

11 "The 5 Biggest Regrets Entrepreneurs Face," Jayson DeMers's website, October 6, 2020, https://jaysondemers.medium.com/the-5-biggest-regrets-entrepreneurs-face-e227f4f29000

12 "How to Live Life Without Major Regrets: 8 Lessons from Older Americans," A. Pawlowski, TODAY, updated December 31, 2019, https://www.today.com/health/biggest-regrets-older-people-share-what-they-d-do-differently-t118918

margin of an American business is just 7.71 percent.[13] This is well below the 10 to 15 percent we recommend maintaining.

A low profit margin often results in a lack of adequate reinvestment into the business, the inability to hire and/or give raises, and the business owner having to do more. A low net profit margin is often a sign that a company is using an ineffective cost structure and/or poor pricing strategies.

Even though many entrepreneurs have low profit margins, many work more hours than they would prefer. According to the Bureau of Labor Statistics, employed people spent 7.6 hours per day working in 2020.[14] Yet in all career fields, the average worker is productive just 60 percent or less of the time at work each day. Office workers are even less productive; the average office worker is productive for only 2 hours and 23 minutes each day.[15]

The truth is, three to four hours of continuous, undisturbed deep work each day is all it takes to see a transformational change in our productivity and our lives. By employing the strategies in this book, you can achieve that work–life balance that you dreamed of when you launched your business. You can reclaim your personal time, your health, and your ability to connect deeply with your spouse.

---

13 "Small Business Profit Margin: What's Considered Good, Bad and Average?" Barb Weidner, FastCapital360, updated November 22, 2021, https://www.fastcapital360.com/blog/net-profit-margin/

14 "American Time Use Survey, May to December 2019 and 2020 Results," Bureau of Labor Statistics press release, July 22, 2021, https://www.bls.gov/news.release/pdf/atus.pdf

15 "15 Employee Productivity Statistics You Want to Know (2022)," Apollo Technical, May 6, 2021, https://www.apollotechnical.com/employee-productivity-statistics/

HOW COMMON IS DIVORCE AMONG ENTREPRENEURS?

Recent statistics about the marital status of small-business owners are scarce. In 2017, the Kauffman Foundation reported that around 71 percent of all entrepreneurs were married. Some divorce lawyers estimate that entrepreneur divorce rate is 5 or 10 percent higher than the divorce rate in the general population, which is typically around 50 percent.

But luckily, one researcher does focus on studying how entrepreneurship affects relationships. Trisha Harp, founder of the Harp Family Institute (HFI), conducts research in this area, revealing that money and intimacy issues are the most common roadblocks to harmony among couples in business, either together or separately. She says 87 percent of entrepreneurs surveyed reported having cash-flow problems at some point in their new careers. As they worked to overcome those financial difficulties, these couples reported that their intimacy decreased significantly.[16]

The good news is, when Harp asked entrepreneurs' spouses if they would still marry the entrepreneur even after they knew this painful truth, 88 percent said yes. She notes that embarking on the entrepreneurial journey tends to bring couples closer together, offsetting some of the issues they experience as a result of working together in some capacity.[17]

Other research seems to confirm that money and intimacy problems top the list of issues that married couples face.

---

16 "Should Entrepreneur Divorce Rate Scare You?" Sylvia Smith, marriage.com, updated September 12, 2017, https://www.marriage.com/advice/divorce/should-entrepreneur-divorce-rate-scare-you/

17 Ibid.

A study by the Austin Institute for The Study of Family and Culture reported that the top reasons for divorce in the United States were infidelity by either party, one spouse being unresponsive to the other's needs, incompatibility; spouse immaturity, emotional abuse, and financial problems.[18] That study was conducted among couples in general—not among couples in business—but the results are still similar.

If you and your spouse are in business together or you both work, you are most likely familiar with the unique challenges couples in business face. The strategies we offer in this book can help you identify and overcome them—together—to build a business, build a marriage, and succeed at both.

LEARN FROM OUR MISTAKES AND SUCCESSES

We've walked a mile in your shoes as a couple who owns and runs a business together. We developed the strategies and guidance in this book, and in our consulting program, based on our own personal experiences together and, over time, on the knowledge we have gained while working with other couples.

You will save time, energy, and potential headaches when you learn from our mistakes. The tools we've created enable entrepreneurial couples—like you—to thrive and prosper under any circumstances. Over time, we have refined our strategies for powering up your business and marriage.

18 "10 Most Common Reasons for Divorce," Shellie R. Warren, marriage.com, updated July 14, 2021, https://www.marriage.com/advice/divorce/10-most-common-reasons-for-divorce/

We want to stress that just because we're coaching other couples doesn't mean we're perfect! We work on our business and marriage every day, and we believe all couples can benefit from doing the same.

To further support you in your journey toward work–marriage balance, we have written a workbook to accompany this book. At the end of each chapter in this book, you will see prompts to click the QR code so you can watch a video and download the workbook.

Let's get started! In chapter 1, we set the stage for the strategies in this book by sharing a bit of our journey with you.

The concepts we have discussed so far apply to just about every couple, whether one or both partners work in the same business or in different businesses. In the next chapter, we will look at two types of couples in business more closely—*solopreneurs* and *couplepreneurs*.

TANDEM BIKE CHECK

Scan the QR code shown below, or visit thetandembook.com/chapter-2, to watch a short video of us discussing this chapter. Also, you can download a free digital workbook that will help you create better balance in business and marriage.

Chapter 3

SOLOPRENEURS AND COUPLEPRENEURS

Whether or not you and your spouse work together, your business is for both of you.

"The goal in marriage is not to think alike, but to think together." | Robert C. Dodds

Whether or not you work with your spouse, the key to building a successful marriage is to have a shared vision and common goals—to work like a team. In this chapter, we identify two types of entrepreneur couples, the challenges they face, and sample solutions.

1. **Couplepreneur**—couples who work together in the same business

2. **Solopreneur**—one spouse who runs a business while the spouse works either in his or her own business, has a separate career, or is a stay-at-home parent

Terms used to describe couples aren't always consistent in the business community. For example, some researchers refer to couples who are in business together as *copreneurs*. But again, for ease of discussion, in this book, we are keeping the nomenclature specific—*couplepreneurs* and *solopreneurs*—to avoid confusion.

We help both types of entrepreneur couples, but most of our clients are couplepreneurs. They work together in some capacity. In many cases, one person works in a business full time, and the spouse helps in that business, either full or part time.

RESOLVING CONFLICT IS A NECESSARY SKILL FOR ALL OF US

Whether or not you and your spouse work together in business, conflict management and resolution is a valuable skill. In fact, this is one of the most valuable skills you can ever use to power up your marriage and business.

We can't imagine that anyone *enjoys* conflict, but many people do everything in their power to avoid it. A healthier strategy is to learn how to *manage and resolve* conflict instead of running from it. This is true in both work and personal relationships. And it's true for both solopreneurs and couplepreneurs.

First, let's look at the high cost of unresolved conflict in the workplace.

Conflict, when managed well, can lead to productive discussions about how to improve processes. It also can lead to innovation, discovery, and progress that might not surface without the nurturing of opposing viewpoints.

But when conflict is not managed well, it is costly to organizations, in terms of staff turnover, loss of productivity, low morale, and other factors.

Even before the COVID-19 pandemic, which forced a high percentage of employees to work remotely beginning in 2020, conflict ate away at organizational profits. It might seem like conflicts would ease once people began working from home, but that's not the case at all.

A 2021 study revealed that 80 percent of remote professionals have experienced workplace conflict. The survey found that most workers (65 percent) experienced conflict with their coworkers. Fights with bosses were a distant second (19 percent). The top four sources of these conflicts were work stress (25 percent), lack of teamwork (25 percent), rude behavior (22 percent), and lack of transparency/honesty about something important (18 percent).[19]

Conflict is just as damaging to our personal relationships. It is unrealistic to expect that we can know someone on a long-term basis without ever disagreeing. And what a boring world it would be if everyone agreed on everything.

Kay Lee and I learned conflict-resolution skills during our two years of premarital counseling. They have been extremely valuable in helping us achieve marriage–work balance and in guiding our clients toward more harmonious interactions at work and at home.

19 "80% of Remote Professionals Have Experienced Workplace Conflict," Jerene Ang, HumanResourcesOnline, February 23, 2021, https://www.humanresourcesonline.net/80-of-remote-professionals-have-experienced-workplace-conflict

How would you and your spouse rate your ability to resolve conflict? How skilled are you and your spouse at managing and resolving conflict? If either one of you avoids conflict at all costs, consider getting help in this area. It will help you communicate and interact much more effectively, both at home and at work.

FEAR OF CONFLICT PREVENTS MANY SOLOPRENEURS FROM WORKING WITH THEIR SPOUSES

A fear of conflict is so prevalent among many business owners that they would never consider asking their spouse to help them in the business. Kay Lee and I ask our solopreneur clients, "Would you ever consider working with your spouse? If you did ask him/her to help you in your business, what would make it work out well for both of you?"

A common response is—without hesitation—"Heck, no! I wouldn't want to work with my spouse."

Many solopreneurs consider that arrangement to be almost taboo. They fear that working together would create conflict.

Over the years, Kay Lee and I have discovered that such a response is often an indicator that those solopreneurs are not skilled at resolving conflict in general. The couple's inability to navigate and resolve conflict is probably already an issue in their marriage.

But if they do know how to resolve conflict, whether or not they work together, they're going to have a healthier marriage. And if they know how to deal with conflict, working together can be very fulfilling and beneficial for the business.

It is possible to derive great fulfillment and happiness by working with your spouse! Going through that journey of launching and growing a business together can bring you closer. We do not want a fear of having conflict in your marriage to be the reason you don't work with your spouse.

Whether or not you work together in the same business is up to you. But the fear of conflict should not be the reason not to. Consider seeking help to resolve conflict. It will be healthy for your marriage and will allow you to work well together, if you choose to.

I admit it—I used to be one of those solopreneurs who didn't want my wife working with me in my business because I feared it would create conflict between us. As with most couples, Kay Lee and I have different backgrounds and different ways of doing things. I envisioned that creating problems and arguments in the business.

When I first started my consulting business, Kay Lee used to ask me, "What can I help you with?"

My response was always, "Nothing."

But then I realized that we already had different ways of doing things at home. We made a good team when it came to getting things done in our personal lives. So why was I resisting her offer to help me in my business? Plus, we had learned how to manage and resolve conflict during our two years of premarital counseling, so we had the tools we needed to navigate any conflicts that arose.

Kay Lee kept prodding me for several months. I finally decided to give her small tasks to see how well we could work together. It actually worked out great, so I began to give her more responsibilities.

She has always excelled at interacting with people; she makes friends easily. I finally came to my senses and realized that her relational skills could be a huge help in the business. That was her superpower. So one day, I told her, "Just go make friends."

When I first told her that, she just looked at me and responded, "That's it? You just want me to go make friends?" She didn't get it at first. Making friends was her superpower, and it's a great sales skill. Even though I excelled in sales in my career, I am an introvert at heart, and it can be a struggle for me to be that outgoing.

Kay Lee can be in the line at Starbucks, and while I'm focused on placing my order, paying, and getting out of there, Kay Lee is chatting people up and making friends. In just a couple of minutes she know all kinds of things about the people she just met while standing in line. She has found out all their kids' and pets' names. At networking events, it is fascinating to watch her in action. She will meet people, find out a little about them, and bring them over to meet me. Not surprisingly, we have obtained clients that way.

KNOW YOUR AND YOUR SPOUSE'S STRENGTHS AND WEAKNESSES

Another area that is important to solopreneurs, couplepreneurs, and anyone else is knowing your strengths and weaknesses, as well as those of the people close to you.

The previous example about Kay Lee's superpower is an example of recognizing and working with each other's strengths.

We believe everyone can benefit from knowing what their strengths and weaknesses are. One resource to help you with this is an assessment offered by Gallup called "Clifton Strengths." (Originally, it was branded as "Clifton StrengthsFinder.") Completing the online talent assessment is your way to discover what you naturally do best, learn how to develop your greatest talents into strengths, and use your personalized results and reports to maximize your potential.[20]

It can help you excel at work and in your personal life. Many times, when husbands and wives work together, conflict arises because one spouse is not in a position that suits his or her strengths. At home or work, our strengths can conflict with our spouse's weaknesses. For example, I can be very decisive, while Kay Lee needs time to ponder. This creates tension because I want to move on something quickly, but she doesn't want to be rushed. Can you hear the ensuing argument?

I recall a situation in which one of our couplepreneur clients had a lot of arguments over personnel matters. The wife, who was the CEO, had taken on that role, but human resources was not her strong area. So we had the husband take on HR because he had better interpersonal skills and the temperament to deal with employee matters. Not only did this resolve the conflict between the two of them; the staff members were much happier as well.

Another resource we find helpful is the DiSC® profile. We typically ask our clients to fill out that assessment, which can help improve

20 "Live Your Best Life Using Your Strengths," Gallup, https://www.gallup.com/cliftonstrengths/en/252137/home.aspx

teamwork, communication, and productivity in the workplace and to help build stronger, more effective working relationships. DiSC is an acronym that stands for the four main personality profiles described in the DiSC model: (D)ominance, (i)nfluence, (S)teadiness, and (C)onscientiousness.[21]

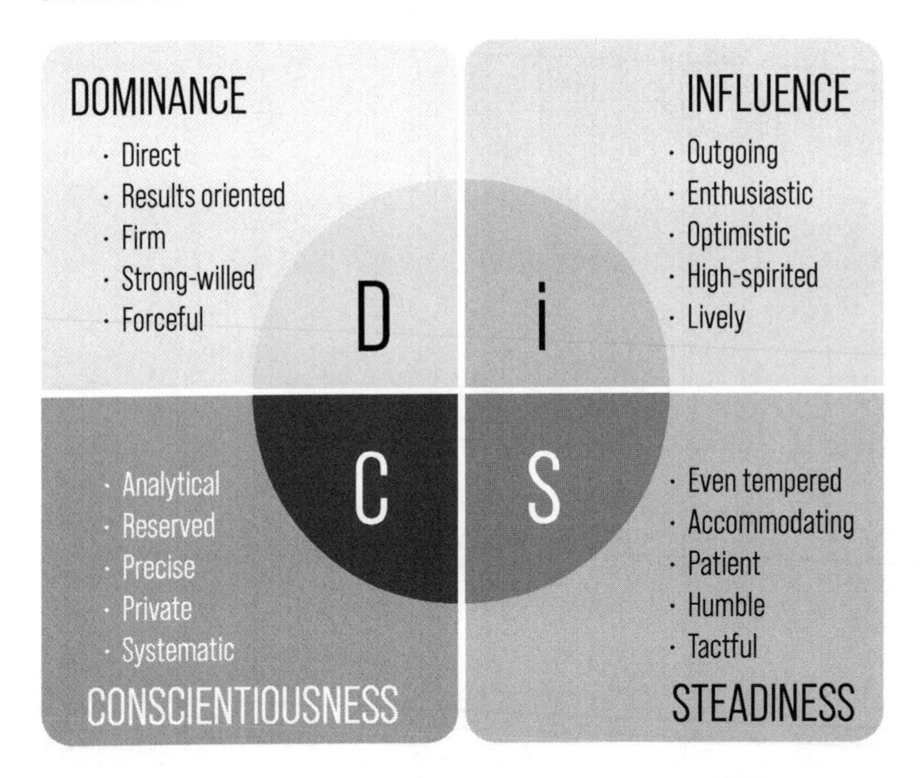

Quite a few times, this assessment has revealed that a business owner or the spouse is working in a role that is not well suited to their personality and work style. Once we know what makes people "tick" using this information, it's easier to discover which roles are ideal for them.

21 "What Is DiSC?" DiSCProfile.com, https://www.discprofile.com/what-is-disc.

It also helps us understand how their personalities can create synergy and where they can create conflict. Remember Kay Lee's superpower of making friends anywhere? That is the high "I" in her, according to the DiSC profile. It's a great attribute for a salesperson. I'm a high "C," so market research, financial analysis, and business planning are my sweet spots.

We clearly have different yet complimentary traits that work well in business and marriage. However, it can create conflict when Kay Lee wants to wing it and I want a plan. My wanting a plan may make her feel like I'm trying to hold her back, while her spontaneity may make me think she's being reckless. You can see how that creates opportunity for conflict.

That's why it's important to understand that our different strengths are great when we work together, but they can tear us apart if we forget that we're on the same team. Like any strong team, we have to learn to appreciate each other's gifts and respect the roles we're in. Doing so enables us to move forward in tandem.

When you are well-suited for a role, you will enjoy it more, perform it better, and be happier and probably healthier, with less conflict.

How do your differences complement each other? In what way do your differences create conflict? What are your strengths and weaknesses? What are your spouse's strengths and weaknesses? How do you, or could you, complement each other in the same work environment? Consider taking the DiSC profile to find out for sure.

KNOW YOUR PARTNER'S "LOVE LANGUAGE," AND EXPRESS WHAT YOURS IS

Yet another area that is important for solopreneurs, couplepreneurs, and anyone else is to know what your significant other's "love language" and what yours is.

Maybe you know about a best-selling book published in 1992 titled *The Five Love Languages: How to Express Heartfelt Commitment to Your Mate*. In that book, the author, Gary Chapman, describes five general ways in which romantic partners express and experience love. He calls them the "love languages," and he says each of us, in general, prefers to receive from our significant other attention in one of those five "languages": words of affirmation, quality time, receiving gifts, acts of service, and physical touch.[22]

It is important to know your spouse's love language. It's equally as important for your spouse to know *your* love language.

> Love languages were the focal point of our work with Benjamin, one of our early clients who participated in our pilot program, Power Couples by Design™. Benjamin has an estate-planning practice, and his wife was a nurse educator for a hospital. He shared with us that while he was growing his business, he would sometimes say to his wife, "Sometimes I feel like I'm alone in this journey of being a business owner."

---

22 Gary Chapman, *The Five Love Languages: How to Express Heartfelt Commitment to Your Mate* (Chicago: Northfield Publishing, 1992). On Gary Chapman's website, at www.5lovelanguages.com, you can take a quiz to discover what your love language is.

She would get upset and tell him, "What do you mean you feel alone? I'm here!" She would make lunch for him, take it to his office, and run errands for him. That was her way of supporting him—through acts of service.

But Benjamin's primary love language was words of affirmation. No matter how many things his wife *did* for him, what he longed for most was to *hear her tell him* that she respected and supported him. He felt lonely because he was not receiving emotional support from his wife, even though she felt she was providing him with that support. They were both unaware of what their partner needed and valued most.

Benjamin needed his wife to listen to him, support him, and communicate her support on an emotional level. Once they both discovered their respective love languages, they understood each other much better. And at that point, his wife finally understood what he meant when he said, "I feel like I'm alone in this business." He was talking about *emotional* loneliness, not *physical* loneliness.

Understanding love languages, and communicating with each other about their own needs, was a turning point for them. It can power up your business and marriage as well.

This is an example of how the spouse who is not working in the business can be of valuable support. That person doesn't need to know anything about the business or work in the business. Yet his or her emotional support can mean the world to the loneliness that many entrepreneurs feel.

What is your primary love language—words of affirmation, quality time, receiving gifts, acts of service, or physical touch? And what is your spouse's love language? If you aren't sure, discuss this with each other.

SOLOPRENEURS: SHARE HIGHLIGHTS OF YOUR BUSINESS LIFE WITH YOUR SPOUSE TO COMBAT ISOLATION

One of the most common issues we see with solopreneurs is that they often experience isolation. There are two main reasons for this:

1. Some business owners don't want to share information about their business life with the spouse. They either think the spouse won't understand or care—in fact, the spouse *doesn't* care or want to understand! Or maybe the business owner doesn't want to burden the spouse with business issues.

2. Some solopreneurs don't want to share what's going on in the business, even when the spouse *does* want to know. Some entrepreneurs want to keep their business successes and challenges to themselves, separate from their home lives. Others are simply exhausted after living out the scenarios at work, and when they get home, they don't want to go through all of it again with the partner.

Neither scenario is healthy for the business or the marriage. Both create distance between the partners.

We recommend sharing key details about your business with your spouse, at some level. You don't have to go deep into the weeds and details. But sharing important developments shows your spouse that you respect him or her and want that person in the loop.

This is what the Heart & Family Institute in Florida advises as well. Although many entrepreneurs believe they are helping their marriages by keeping their work lives to themselves, the institute says the opposite is true. They write, "Contrary to what one might believe, the Heart's data showed that when entrepreneurs shared both positive and negative aspects of the business on a regular basis, the other spouse's trust and confidence in the entrepreneur actually increased. Sharing on a regular basis increases the spouse's belief in their entrepreneur's ability to succeed."[23]

HOW KAY LEE AND I SOLVED OUR ISOLATION ISSUE

When I was winding down my corporate career, I was that solopreneur who didn't want to share details about my day with Kay Lee. At that time, she was launching a home-based interior design business. She was home by herself most of the time. As soon as I walked in the door, she would ask how my day went.

I would respond with, "It was good."

My cryptic response would leave Kay Lee feeling left out and shut down. But I didn't intend to hurt her feelings; it's just that I had been talking and trying to close sales all day. Once I got home, I just wanted to unwind. As an introvert, it was exhausting for me to be around people all day. I needed time to decompress.

23 "Is Your Marriage to an Entrepreneur Doomed?" Darrah Brustein, *Entrepreneur*, June 3, 2016, https://www.entrepreneur.com/article/276449

The key was that we discussed this issue. We shared our frustrations with one another, and then we discussed a strategy for getting on the same page.

We agreed that, when I first got home from work, I would change clothes and then take the dog for a walk. This would give me about half an hour to decompress. Then, when I returned to the house, we could talk about my day. That was an easy solution that satisfied both of us. But we could not have gotten there without discussing it.

This kind of discussion is vital because as long as it is left undiscussed, it will fester and get worse. When a business owner faces financial issues at work and keeps the details from the spouse, that causes uncertainty and fear to creep into the spouse's mind. But when you share key details on a regular basis, it helps calm those fears and maintain trust. It's all about sharing your journey with your spouse—whether or not he or she works with you in the business.

Sharing the highlights helps ease the conflict and loneliness.

In the next section, we will switch gears and discuss couplepreneurs and some of the challenges they face, more so than solopreneurs.

COMMON CHALLENGES COUPLEPRENEURS FACE

Couplepreneurs—couples who work in the same business together—face some of the same challenges as solopreneurs, but they also have challenges that are unique to their situation. You'll recognize this first one—we just discussed the importance of knowing you and your spouse's strengths and weaknesses.

1. **Putting the spouse in a role he or she isn't good at and/or doesn't want.** We all know that when launching a business,

> entrepreneurs end up wearing all the hats and doing some tasks they are not good at and don't enjoy. Then, if the time comes when they decide to ask their spouse to work in the business, they often put him or her in a role that he or she isn't good at and/or doesn't want to fill. Often, that is an administrative or bookkeeping role. The business owner begins to offload those mundane but essential administrative tasks to the spouse. That works well only if that's a role the spouse is good at and wants to fill.

Research shows that in businesses started by married men, 60 percent of them had their spouses take on a business support role, such as administrative work, to help the business succeed. In contrast, in businesses launched by women, the spouse was involved in the business only 35 percent of the time.

When a spouse is expected to do work he or she isn't good at and doesn't enjoy, it becomes frustrating. Then the business owner becomes frustrated because the quality of work isn't what he or she was expecting. This often creates conflict.

If your spouse is going to work in the business, it's important to have open, honest discussions, in advance, about the types of work he or she does and does not want to do. If there are roles that both you and your spouse don't want to do, consider hiring someone.

For example, Kay Lee and I both dread doing QuickBooks® and accounting. So we are working on hiring someone to handle those tasks for us.

This is an area where open, honest discussion is needed—and sometimes conflict resolution. We have worked with clients who were afraid to tell their spouses they did not enjoy the roles they were in. They didn't want to create conflict, so they just suffered silently. That's not healthy for anyone! Not only that—resentment begins to build up in that scenario.

2. **Failing to define roles and responsibilities clearly.** Once you and your spouse agree on which role(s) he or she will fill, the next step is to outline exactly what types of duties you will expect to be done. We all need clear guidelines about what's expected of us, whether in the workplace or at home. We can't meet one another's expectations if we have no idea what they are!

3. **Failing to have regular business meetings.** Scheduling regular meetings makes it easier for both of you to set boundaries between your work-related and personal issues. If you don't schedule regular meetings, it's too easy for work issues to become the main topic at dinner or when you're trying to enjoy down time together. Establishing work–marriage balance requires that you create boundaries between these two aspects of your life; don't let them blur together. Otherwise, work is sure to consume your life.

Kay Lee and I have our weekly business meetings on Monday afternoons at 3:30. We start each meeting by stating something we admire and love about each other. Kay Lee is great about encouraging me regularly, but I'm terrible at encouraging her. Starting our meetings that way gets me in the habit of encouraging her, and it and makes each meeting something we both look forward to. We discuss the week, the month, and even the rest of the year. We discuss client projects and priorities, and we check in with each other on our business goals. These meetings are critical because they enable us to leave work at work so that when we go home, we are focused on our marriage, not on the business.

Our weekly Monday-afternoon meetings have helped us work well together in business and marriage. If you are part of a couplepreneur, how solid is the boundary between your work and your marriage? Do you have regular work meetings to prevent work issues from seeping into your time at home together?

In our work with clients, we have never concluded that couples shouldn't work together. We believe anyone can work together, as long as they understand their and their spouse's strengths and weaknesses—and take on roles that are suitable for them. They also need to know the best way to resolve inevitable conflict.

Please resist the urge to put your spouse in the role where you need help the most, just to fill a seat with free or inexpensive labor!

AN EXAMPLE OF COUPLEPRENEURS WHO WORK WELL TOGETHER

We want to describe a couple who works extremely well together so you can envision what an ideal scenario might look like.

Kay Lee and I interviewed a couple named Phil and Dana Liberatore on episode 52 of our podcast, "Power Up Your Marriage and Business." They own a tax and accounting firm. Phil had started the business before they met. He has a degree in accounting and finance, and Dana is an ordained minister. They had very different backgrounds and talents, so working together effectively would require some thought and strategy about how best to go about it.

Once they got married, Dana eventually began helping Phil in the business. She is essentially the chief operating officer and is in charge of all the structure, policies, and procedures for the business. Phil is like Kay Lee—he is skilled at networking and bringing in clients. He is the chief rainmaker for the business.

Phil is the visionary—he comes up with great ideas, and Dana figures out how to implement them. He is a likeable person, but he is not as gifted at creating order in the business as Dana—even though he is an accountant. He will be the first one to tell you that if it weren't for Dana, their business would not be as successful as it is. And even though Dana had no background in accounting, she excels at organization and systems, which are crucial for any business.

They make a highly effective team. They allow each other to fill their respective roles and do their respective jobs the way they think is best.

We like the example that Phil and Dana set because their success is proof that spouses don't have to have the same knowledge, education, and background to succeed in a business together.

Go to www.marriedentrepreneur.co and access that podcast interview from our website, free of charge.

The lesson here? When you recognize each other's differences and celebrate them, as opposed to letting them create conflict, you'll be a winning team.

TANDEM BIKE CHECK

Scan the QR code shown below, or visit thetandembook.com/chapter-3, to watch a short video of us discussing this chapter. Also, you can download a free digital workbook that will help you create better balance in business and marriage.

Chapter 4

GET ON THE SAME PAGE

To get on the same page, write your vision down on one page.

"Create a vision for the life you really want, and then work relentlessly towards making it a reality." | Roy T. Bennett

Achieving a healthy balance between work and marriage is a major theme of this book. And the first step to improving that balance is *getting on the same page*. Accomplishing that requires that you create your *vision* as a couple.

ESTABLISH A VISION FOR YOUR MARRIAGE

In business, most of us are accustomed to establishing a vision, setting goals, and striving to reach them. Successful business owners write business plans, marketing plans, sales plans, and recruiting plans. That's critical because without a clear vision and purpose, it's difficult to know what you want the business to achieve. It's also difficult to keep everyone associated with the business on the same page, striving for the same goals and outcome. Having no targets to shoot for is as bad as having too many.

Similarly, financial advisors lead their clients to write down their financial goals and priorities, estimate the costs associated with them, and then develop a budget to keep their spending on track so they can reach their goals. Documenting your priorities and end goals is incredibly important. Keep in mind that your priorities can change over time, as you navigate life transitions and as unexpected situations arise.

Having a vision is just as important for your marriage, yet most couples don't discuss a vision for the future of their marriage and family. They may talk about it from time to time, but that's not the same as having formal discussion about how you will achieve your goals and writing them down.

John Assaraf, who owns five multibillion-dollar companies, believes so strongly in creating a vision that he makes this bold statement: **"Without a clear and precise vision of exactly what it is you want, you'll never reach it or have it."**

Assaraf is the founder and CEO of NeuroGym, a company dedicated to using the most advanced technologies and evidence based brain training methods to help individuals unleash their fullest potential and maximize their results. He points to science to explain that we can manifest whatever we focus on. In a 2021 blog post, he discusses the research and science behind this concept:

Whatever we focus on and emotionalize often is what we will attract and actually see in the quantum field of all possibilities, or better yet, probabilities...Since all material things move from the non-physical to the physical reality, our vision and goals are paramount in the process of achievement. Our vision and focus acts like a magnet that attracts and connects the pieces together... It's the clear and consistent vibration of your vision that brings forth your needs. You provide the seed, the universe provides the resources. Therefore, you must now make your "new vision" inside your brain more real than the current results in your outside world.[24]

This seems to be the biblical version of Matthew 17:20: "Truly I tell you, if you have faith as small as a mustard seed, you can say to this mountain, 'Move from here to there,' and it will move. Nothing will be impossible for you.'"

It's hard to work well together in life and business when you haven't defined your direction together. Dream big, and write down your shared life vision.

Imagine what a powerful exercise it will be for you and your spouse to create a vision of the future together! People aren't as inclined to do this exercise for their marriage, but we encourage you to do so. It will give you a road map, a guideline, for making decisions as you both reach important milestones regarding family, finances, and work.

24 John Assaraf, blog post titled "The Power of Having a Vision: How Quantum Physics, Your Brain, and Your Heart Manifest Your Vision and Goals," JohnAssaraf.com, date unknown, https://www.johnassaraf.com/the-power-of-having-a-vision/

Because of the culture we live in, we tend to prioritize business and try to figure out how to fit our family life into the business. But when we establish a vision as a couple or family, decide on priorities together, and strive toward common goals in an intentional way, we turn that equation around. Now we are fitting work life into family life. We have made family life a priority instead of relegating it to the "back burner."

YOU CAN'T ACHIEVE WHAT YOU CAN'T DEFINE

When we interviewed best-selling author and former Dave Ramsey personality Christy Wright on our podcast, "Power Up Your Marriage and Business," she said something I haven't forgotten.

Better work–life balance is the number one issue entrepreneurs ask her about. They want better balance in their lives, but the problem is they haven't defined what it is or what it should look like in their lives. They know they don't have it, and they want it, but they can't define it.

As achievers, we can obtain what we set our minds to, but we need to know what it looks like. Otherwise, how do we know how to get it and that we have it when we get it?

So the first step in achieving greater work–life balance is for you and your spouse to define what it looks like for you. There is no cookie-cutter solution to this because everyone's life and business situation is different.

It's a bit easier for us to take workcations because we have no kids and our business is virtual. But if you own a restaurant and have four kids, things get a bit more complicated. We get it, so we don't expect balance in your life to look like ours. But we do know things can be better once you agree on what winning in business and marriage could look like.

TO GET ON THE SAME PAGE, WRITE YOUR VISION DOWN ON ONE PAGE

Now, talking about your vision for the future and your priorities is essential, but that alone isn't enough. You need to write your vision and goals down on paper. You don't have to write a lot, but you do need to write it down.

To get on the same page, we recommend writing down your vision on one page. Brainstorm what you want the future of your marriage to look like. What do you both dream of experiencing and accomplishing? What is most important to you?

Once you have an idea of what that looks like, build a practical, step-by-step plan for how you can accomplish those things—now, in the short term, and in the long term. To determine your short-term priorities as a couple, ask yourselves "How do we want to live our lives?" To determine your long-term priorities—your vision—ask yourselves, "What do we want to work toward together?"

Kay Lee and I both love to travel, and our long-term vision as a couple includes owning two homes someday. I love the mountains, snow, and skiing, and Kay Lee loves the beach. She likes to ski, too, but she would prefer to spend time at the beach. Having one home in the mountains and one at the beach would enable us to have the best of both worlds together.

As we get older, we will probably still engage in consulting. We love what we do. But in the long term, we will probably shift our focus more to mentoring entrepreneur couples and investing in their businesses. That would require less of our time commitment on a daily basis but still keep us heavily invested in our clients' businesses. We also want to coach other coaches who want to help entrepreneur couples.

We plan to travel more once we make that shift from regular consulting to investing and mentoring. But we don't want to wait that long to travel! So in the short term, we have become intentional about building our business so we can take "workcations" together.

For example, last November, we planned to travel to South Dakota to visit clients. Instead of flying, we decided to drive and make a road trip out of it so we could stop at some national parks. Soon after that, we traveled to Charlotte, North Carolina, to visit a client who is a NASCAR driver. We watched him race, met with him, and then spent an extra two weeks in the area. We got to hang out in Myrtle Beach and Hilton Head and see the fall colors in the Smoky Mountains.

One of our yearly plans is to take these workcations in addition to our quarterly weekenders and our annual big vacations.

Because we have identified travel as part of our marriage vision, we take advantage of opportunities to mix travel with client visits. We are doing this intentionally, and it helps keep us on the same page and allows us to have fun in the journey of building the business. The plan should not be so rigid and focused on achievement that you forget to have fun.

As you focus on those priorities that compose your vision, you will find it easier to attain marriage–work balance. While focusing on the priorities and cutting out everything else, your personal life and work life will start to become better organized.

Creating your vision together as a couple makes it easier to manage the constant power struggle that couples face. Deciding together on your priorities as a couple gives you both a reference point when disagreements arise. For example, if you receive an unexpected sale or bonus, and the two of you disagree about how to spend or invest it, review your vision. What does it say about your priorities? That vision serves to guide every decision you make together, whether it's related to time, money, or something else.

HAVING A COMMON VISION MAKES IT EASIER TO SET BOUNDARIES AND BE PRESENT

While we were working on our vision and adjusting the business to run more efficiently to increase our margin of time, we created better balance in our lives by setting proper boundaries between work and home.

When we don't set boundaries, we end up just letting life happen to us, and we are not likely to achieve marriage–work balance. By setting boundaries, we can keep from letting the business become the "mistress."

Setting boundaries and prioritizing activities requires that we make good use of the time we have. The busy entrepreneur works a lot of hours as it is. So when we're home, it's important that we are present with our spouse and family. We can be home physically but not there mentally or emotionally. That creates distance between spouses.

Our office is located at home, so separating work from home can be even more challenging. It's too easy to check that email one more time or fine-tune another sales projection. And then there's the phone—you know how it is. You get that text, email, or "emergency" phone call during dinner.

Those are things that keep us away from giving our undivided attention to each other. Even while we were working to create more margin in our lives, it was important for Kay Lee and me to give each other our best with the time we had. It was surprising to find that even when we didn't have more time to give to each other, the *quality* of time we spent together went up, and our relationship benefited.

Sit down with your spouse and write out your vision for the future as a couple. Your vision will establish your priorities, which will make it easier to set boundaries on your focus and time.

Kay Lee and I have agreed on boundaries that help us keep our work life separate from our personal life. Here are four of them:

1. We do not work on nights and weekends. Now, sometimes that is unavoidable, but we plan for it. If we have to work on a Saturday, for example, we will take the next Monday off.
2. We will not take calls or text anyone at or beyond dinner time.
3. We do not visit our social media sites on Saturdays.
4. We do not talk business on personal time. We discuss any work-related issues during our Monday-afternoon business meetings.

Now, we're not so rigid with the rules that there is no room for latitude, but we do hold each other accountable to these basic boundaries. Agreeing to these boundaries, and abiding by them, helps keep us on the same page and stay connected. Following these guidelines makes it easier for us to enjoy quality time together.

What boundaries have you and your spouse established to preserve your quality time? If you have not established any, discuss this topic, and create your list of boundaries that will help you separate your work life and personal life.

BE INTENTIONAL ABOUT GETTING ON THE SAME PAGE

Creating better balance between marriage and work requires that you are both *intentional* about the process and that you work together to develop a plan of action for your lives, both inside and outside the business. Being intentional simply requires that you define what's important and then make it happen.

I (Kay Lee) am extremely conscious about making time with Robert a priority because I have experienced a lot of frustration with my dad about finding time to get together.

My dad, my sister, and I will talk about going out to lunch. We will ask Dad, "So when are we going to meet, and at what time?"

He will say, "Oh, I don't know. I'll just call you." But the next day comes, and he doesn't call us. I will tell him, "Dad, we need to make a specific plan because we have a lot going on."

When I finally do get him to agree on a time and place, he sometimes cancels on me at the last minute because a friend is in town. This frustrates me because "quality time" is my love language, and it is difficult to spend time with him. It also makes me feel like he doesn't value me because he decides to spend time with someone else. This situation also makes me feel like I'm wasting valuable time and energy that I could be devoting to something else.

Clearly, my dad and I are not on the same page! I have tried to talk with him about this, but he doesn't say much. He just doesn't want to deal with it. Clearly, quality time is not his love language.

We see this scenario play out with couples, too. Both people are extremely busy and focused on their own priorities. Life comes at us fast, and if we are not *intentional* about how we spend our time and energy, we can end up exhausted and frustrated, with not much to show for it. Establishing your vision as a couple encourages you both to be intentional about making each other a priority. Setting that vision together, and then agreeing to follow it, helps couples be more intentional about spending more time together.

SCHEDULE QUALITY TIME TOGETHER ON YOUR CALENDARS

Even if "quality time" is not your love language, spending time together as a couple is important for your relationship.

Kay Lee's love language is "quality time," but my love language is "receiving gifts." I know that spending quality time together is important for her to feel connected to me. So, even if "quality time" isn't my love language, it needs to be important to me if it's important to her because we are a couple. It's not about me or her; it's about *us*. It's about what is healthy for our relationship.

Now, let's be clear: being at home together or at work together, focused on something besides each other, doesn't count as *quality* time!

A recent study found that couples who make time to do activities that required interacting together, such as playing board games or taking a painting class together, also had a good-quality love life.

The researchers wrote that partners who took part in these fun activities together saw an increase in oxytocin, which is often called the "love hormone" because it plays a key role in bonding behaviors. Interacting together is crucial; simply attending an event together but not interacting may not have the same bonding effect. The researchers also found that the novelty factor influenced how much oxytocin they released: Couples who organized their fun activity in a new place outside their home saw a greater oxytocin boost than those who played at home. The researchers' takeaway was that doing fun things together—ideally in new, unfamiliar surroundings—might help maintain relationship quality.[25]

One practical way to make sure you spend quality time together is to share/sync your calendars with one another. Because Kay Lee and I can access each other's calendars, it's easy for us to set aside time for the priorities we have set together. We are very intentional about it. If we don't set aside that time for date nights, it's easy for other activities to get in the way. Sharing our calendars also keeps us from double-booking appointments or other priorities.

Scheduled check-ins will help you both keep your promise to one another to spend quality time together. It might sound counterintuitive, but we believe you need to plan to be spontaneous. Without a shared intention, couples tend to fill their calendars with every imaginable priority except one another.

To get on the same page, discuss what is important to you both—in the present, in the short term, and in the long term. Then make a plan to make those priorities happen. Put them on the calendar. Be intentional about them.

Do you and your spouse share your calendars? If not, try doing so to make it easier to set aside quality time together.

25 "Why Playing Board Games Could Improve Your Love Life," Katharine Paddock, PhD, MedicalNewsToday, February 14, 2019, https://www.medicalnewstoday.com/articles/324454

When couples don't spend enough time together, they lose their sense of connection. They can drift apart. Sometimes, that can set the stage for a permanent disconnect—divorce.

Laurence Hirsch, an attorney in Arizona who represents clients in high-net-worth divorces, says the number one reason why CEO marriages fail is a lack of time for family. He says—and we agree—that CEOs are almost always at work, and when they're not, they're thinking about work. "What's more, blowback from a bad quarter or PR crisis can consume their attention round-the-clock for weeks," Hirsch writes. "So whenever they are home, their energy, attention, and patience can be in short supply. Over time, spouses may feel taken for granted or unappreciated, especially if they shoulder all the domestic responsibilities, even though they themselves may have a job. You end up with these fractured relationships where the husband and wife are almost living two separate lives."[26]

It can take time and practice to get into the habit of making time for your spouse. This is why we check in with couples. Sometimes, when we ask about their progress, they will say, "Well, we didn't do it so well this week or this month. We didn't have a single date night."

We will ask them, "Why? What got in the way?"

Once we know what the obstacles are that are preventing them from getting on the same page, we can work through it with them. It's a matter of coming up with, and employing, solutions to figure out what's getting in the way and how to remove those obstacles.

---

26 "Being CEO Can Kill a Marriage—Here's How to Prevent That," Jeanne Sahadi, CNN Business, September 30, 2018, https://www.cnn.com/2018/09/30/success/ceo-marriage/index.html

Sometimes, there is a legitimate excuse for missing quality time with each other. But those situations should be exceptions to the rule. In general, you should be able to keep to those date nights.

Prioritize what's most important.

SHARING GOALS LEADS TO HIGHER SATISFACTION AND SUSTAINED LOVE

Trisha Harp, whom we mentioned earlier, has conducted research showing that entrepreneurs who set shared long-term business and family goals with their spouses scored higher in every area of satisfaction than those who didn't. Her surveys have revealed that of those entrepreneurs who set shared business goals with their spouses, 98 percent reported being still in love with their spouse.[27]

Sharing goals can seem difficult at first. But again, doing so is necessary to achieving harmony in your personal life. Of course each person in your family has different interests and dreams. The more people there are in your family, the more important it is for everyone to get on the same page.

A wonderful example of this is a friend of ours who visited us recently in California. She has nine kids, ranging in age from three to twenty. A couple of years ago, they all decided collectively that they wanted to visit friends and family in California together. So they estimated how much money they would need, and the kids who are old enough to work all

27 "Is Your Marriage to an Entrepreneur Doomed?" Darrah Brustein, ThriveGlobal, April 2, 2018, https://medium.com/thrive-global/is-your-marriage-to-an-entrepreneur-doomed-c137d092d0ab

got side jobs and saved money for the trip. There were ten of them, and they all pitched in to achieve the shared goal. They were intentional about it, and they made it happen.

FINANCES ARE A BIG PART OF YOUR PLANNING

In business, it is necessary to estimate the cost of every goal you set that is a part of your vision. It's the same with marriage goals. When you set short- and long-term goals, estimate the costs. For long-term goals, be sure to factor in inflation. As you brainstorm your vision together, finances need to be a part of your planning process.

We recently taught a session on finance in a marriage class at our church because getting on the same page financially is the number one hot topic in most marriages. Disagreements about money are also a top reason for divorce.

In the American Psychological Association's 2020 "Stress in America" survey, 64 percent of adults said money is a significant source of stress in their lives. And because different people often manage money in different ways, conflicts easily arise. One type of financial-related conflict is when one person is a spender and the other is a saver. Another common source of conflict is when one partner agrees to stay home with the kids while the other supports the family financially. After the children are grown, though, the financial supporter often wants the stay-at-home spouse to enter or return to the workforce, but that spouse may be unable or unwilling to find outside work.[28]

28 "5 Reasons Long-Term Marriages Crumble," Robin L. Flanigan, AARP, May 27, 2021, https://www.aarp.org/home-family/friends-family/info-2021/long-term-marriage-and-divorce.html

Too many couples let these major conflicts continue without discussing them. Left unresolved, these and other issues cause resentment to build up. This is why it's critical to address such power struggles early in your marriage by discussing what each of you wants. And then you have to find common ground to ensure that both of you feel like your dreams and desires are being met.

To what extent are you and your spouse on the same page, financially speaking? If you do not have a financial advisor, consider finding one to work with as you plan out the financial aspects of your marriage vision.

HELPING SPENDERS AND SAVERS FIND COMMON GROUND

When a couple's conflict involves the fact that one is a spender and the other is a saver, a lot of emotions surround the issue. For spenders like me, saving money and living by a budget can seem constricting. But for savers like Kay Lee, it means security and confidence about the future. There is nothing wrong with spending money unless it cuts into long-term financial health.

Keep in mind that as you progress toward your long-term vision over time, your financial plan will most likely need to be adjusted. The priorities we are planning for thirty years in advance are probably going to change when we get closer to them. You will discover wants and needs you didn't realize you would have years earlier.

For example, you and your spouse might be on track to fund a comfortable retirement. But then, what if your spouse decides he or she must have a motorcycle? Topics like this require going back to the vision conversation to discuss what you both want for the future and how to make it all happen.

Maybe your spouse wants to finance the motorcycle, but you prefer to save up for it. You will probably want to get your financial advisor involved in this discussion to find out how to adjust your financial plan so you can accommodate the new motorcycle and the comfortable retirement. You can achieve everything you both want, but again, it will probably require compromise and adjustment.

We would be inclined to recommend to this couple that it's better to save and pay cash for the motorcycle as opposed to financing it because the interest payments will cut into their ability to save for future goals. They can buy the motorcycle, but why pay more for it in the way of interest payments? This requires delayed gratification but keeps more money in their pocket for the future.

Once you agree on your vision and goals, it becomes easier to sort out the financial aspect of saving to achieve those goals. Your budget simply becomes the means by which you will achieve your goals and vision.

PLAN YOUR COST AND TIME REQUIREMENTS FOR A VACATION IN ADVANCE

One practical way to accommodate a new need or want financially is to back out of it.

For example, let's say you both decide you want to take a vacation next year that will cost $2,000. How much money do you need to save each month to save up $2,000 by the time you go on vacation? If the vacation is 10 months away, then you'll need to save $200 per month for it. That is probably easily doable.

It might mean cutting out a few lunches or dinners out each month. Or maybe one of you can earn $200 per month in a side hustle. The important thing is, work this out together, and make sure one of you isn't sacrificing more than the other. Again, that is a situation ripe for resentment.

If you are a couplepreneur, you will also need to plan how to keep the business running while you are away on vacation. This is another area where you will need to plan together. It might mean doubling up on work before you leave or hiring someone (or training existing staff) to move projects along while you're gone. You want your business to keep running as usual, even if you're away. You want the business to run smoothly so you don't face a backlog of work or errors that must be fixed once you return. This is also a great way to prepare an employee to take on more or promote them to take the load permanently off someday.

This is one reason entrepreneurs often hesitate to go on vacation—they dread the pile of work that will be waiting for them when they return. But skipping vacations isn't fair to the spouse or family. Again, that's a classic case in which the business can become the "mistress."

The key is advance planning—for the logistics of the vacation, the financial cost, and the workload and staffing aspect.

Whether you are a solopreneur or a couplepreneur, these steps are necessary for getting on the same page with your spouse—creating your vision together, establishing your priorities for the long and short term, budgeting for those priorities, setting boundaries, and compromising to ensure you're both happy.

WHY MANY ENTREPRENEURS RESIST GOING ON VACATION

Entrepreneurs are typically really driven to accomplish, succeed, and win. While that's admirable, this approach often leads to significant imbalance between marriage and work. An important element of powering up your marriage and business is to take regular vacations together. But many resist doing so. Of course every entrepreneur is different, but here are two common reasons why entrepreneurs often resist taking time off work to spend time with their families or to go on vacation.

1. They Have a Hard Time "Letting Go"

Many entrepreneurs feel it necessary to control every aspect of their business. They end up working harder because they find it difficult to delegate routine tasks to other people.

We enjoy guiding our clients through this process. Once entrepreneurs commit to spending more time with their spouses and families, it sort of forces them to go on vacation once in a while, which, in turn, forces them to learn how to delegate work they should have been delegating to someone else all along.

Delegating work to someone else usually means you have to train that person. And then, as you train someone new, you might realize you need to invest in technology to streamline your processes, systems, and operations—maybe a customer relationship management (CRM) system or a bookkeeping app. That can seem like an extra expense and burden, but if it helps you accomplish more in less time, then it's worth the investment.

Making quality time with your family a priority does require advance planning in terms of the time, money, and workload aspects. But in the end, you will be more relaxed, your family will be happy you all spent time together, and you can end up working fewer hours.

Yes, your new staff member or contractor will probably make some mistakes in the beginning. But that's a necessary part of learning. Be patient, and give it time. As your business grows, you can't possibly fill every role in the business. And, as we discussed earlier, you shouldn't attempt to, anyway.

Once your new staff person or contractor has a good grasp of the work involved and you have great new systems in place, it will become easier for you and your spouse to get away for those weekenders, too. Such investments in your business are also investments in your marriage and quality of life. And the business will benefit as well. The less you're involved with the day-to-day details, the better. Everyone will be happier!

2. They Have a Fear of Missing Out (FOMO)

Another hallmark of entrepreneurs is that many of them suffer from FOMO— fear of missing out. They are tuned in to every potential client, deal, sale, or experience. As a result, they often feel like spending time away from the office could mean missed opportunities. This is why it's difficult for many entrepreneurs to say no when they need to. They have a difficult time setting boundaries. (Just try taking an entrepreneur's phone away during dinner!) But again, that is often why they suffer from marriage–work imbalance.

Entrepreneurs often find it difficult to "unplug" and to disconnect from their work, even if they are exhausted. Business is always on their minds. They want to think about it and discuss it. But that constant need to perform ends up working against them. They end up working harder, not smarter. And in many cases, they put their health, well-being, and marriage at risk.

We have a friend (let's call him "Busy Bill") who has to give himself three days to get into vacation mode. What a waste. While he's weaning himself off work mentally, his wife needs to find ways to entertain herself while she tries not to take his lack of presence personally.

This example shows the benefit of "unplugging" weekly, like our Saturday boundaries of no work and no social media. Once you get into a rhythm of unplugging, you won't be like Busy Bill and waste vacation time trying to get into the mood.

STRESS, WORKING TOO MUCH, AND BURNOUT THREATEN ENTREPRENEURS' HEALTH

Rest is incredibly important for our mental, emotional, and physical health.

A March 2021 study from Indeed.com revealed that burnout—a state of emotional, physical and mental exhaustion caused by excessive and prolonged stress—is on the rise among US workers. More than half (52 percent) of survey respondents said they were experiencing burnout—up from the 43 percent who said the same in Indeed's pre-Covid-19 survey. Baby Boomers show a 7 percent increase in burnout, and Gen-Xers saw a 14 percent jump during that year.[29]

29 "Experiencing Burnout? Here's How to Fix It," Kelly Lynn Adams, Entrepreneur, July 2, 2021, https://www.entrepreneur.com/article/375986.

A 2021 survey by the American Psychological Association found that Americans were more stressed out in 2020–21 than in previous years, and that stress has taken a toll on our physical health. More than 40 percent of the survey respondents said they had gained weight during the pandemic, nearly one-fourth said they were drinking more, and nearly two-thirds were sleeping too much or too little. These factors led to a rise in health problems related to weight gain, like diabetes and hypertension. They have also taken a toll on Americans' mental health. One-third of adults reported symptoms of anxiety or depression, and 12 percent had seriously considered suicide in the previous thirty days.[30]

The pandemic took its toll on entrepreneurs specifically as well.

A global study conducted in 2021 revealed that many entrepreneurs felt pandemic-related issues threatened their livelihoods and their mental well-being, largely because they have fewer resources than large businesses. Almost 40 percent (39.7 percent) of entrepreneurs surveyed said they had high levels of uncertainty and unpredictability for their businesses. Only 50 percent found enough time to mentally recover from work. And 61 percent of entrepreneurs saw the very existence of their business under threat in the pandemic. The associated stress also impacted entrepreneurs' self-care, which is critical for maintaining mental health. Only half of entrepreneurs in the study found enough

30 "The Pandemic Has Increased Our Stress Levels, And It's Affecting Our Physical Health," Rhitu Chatterjee, NPR, March 12, 2021, https://www.npr.org/2021/03/12/976342925/the-pandemic-has-increased-our-stress-levels-and-its-affecting-our-physical-heal

time to recover from work stress, and 44 percent reported not getting sufficient sleep.[31]

God, in His infinite wisdom, made the directive to "obey the Sabbath" in the Ten Commandments. God intends for us to take a day off each week. Of course He wants us to spend time with Him, but it's not just a spiritual respite. Taking that day off gives us time to replenish our physical, mental, and emotional strength.

Have you ever resisted going on vacation, or postponed a vacation, because you felt you needed to take care of work issues? If the answer is yes, sit down and write out a plan for getting those issues covered so you can plan a family vacation.

Think about this. Taking time off is so important to God that it's up there with "thou shalt not kill" and "Thou shalt not commit adultery." Maybe it's something we should all take seriously.

Many entrepreneurs wear stress-related exhaustion like a badge of honor. But driving themselves too hard benefits no one. Because the signs of health-related issues due to stress can be invisible, many are on the verge of a heart attack or stroke, without knowing it. Stress is a silent killer. We know clients, friends, family members, and even pastors who have faced burnout because they're constantly on the go—giving, doing, and striving.

31 "Toll of Pandemic on Entrepreneurs' Mental Health Revealed in New Report," King's College London, April 8, 2021, https://www.kcl.ac.uk/news/toll-of-pandemic-on-entrepreneurs-mental-health-revealed-in-new-report

They say yes to everything and everyone. They are not taking care of themselves, their spouses, or their families in an ideal way.

We encourage you to minimize the stress in your life—not only to achieve better marriage–work balance, but also to keep you healthy and strong for years to come. Like anything else, letting go, delegating, taking breaks, and focusing on self-care might not come easy at first. Make it a priority, and you and your spouse can keep each other accountable for daily decisions that impact your health.

So when your spouse says, "It's Sunday morning. You shouldn't be taking that call," he or she isn't nagging you. Instead, your spouse is simply reminding you that the marriage vision you created together lists a healthy lifestyle as a top priority. It's a matter of living life well in the present so you can build for the future.

When you are well rested, your entrepreneurial innovation, creativity, and vision for the future all become clearer. We know it's a struggle to start and build a business. You can get away with pushing yourself too hard for a while, but eventually, it's going to catch up to you. It's not healthy for you as an individual, and it's not healthy for your marriage or for your business.

Have you ever experienced burnout, or are you feeling it now? How does it affect your health, your ability to focus, and your relationships? What can you and will you do to strive for a healthier marriage–work balance?

EFFECTIVE COMMUNICATION IS THE KEY TO GETTING ON THE SAME PAGE

This entire process—sitting down to brainstorm your marriage vision, deciding on your priorities as a couple, setting boundaries, encouraging one another, and holding each other accountable—requires effective communication.

Many couples avoid confrontations—and even discussions—at all costs. (In the next chapter, we discuss conflict resolution, which is critical to getting past that roadblock.) If you are to get on the same page and achieve marriage–work balance, the two of you have to discuss these issues. No one is a mind reader! Sharing what's on your mind will keep the two of you connected and will make your marriage resilient to resentment.

The more uncomfortable a conversation is, the more important it is for you to have it. During your weekly business meetings, be straightforward and honest with each other. The only way to get on the same page is to get all the facts out on the table and discuss them. Then decide how to handle the issue.

Some issues can't and shouldn't wait for your weekly meeting. Kay Lee and I often have impromptu check-ins with each other that last only five or ten minutes. When an issue arises, we need to discuss it right then. These check-ins are quality moments. You are saying to each other, "You're the most important person in my life. I love you. How can I help?"

Everyone can find five or ten minutes for a valuable check-in. And everyone can find an hour and a half for that weekly business meeting.

These are important tools in moving your business forward in a way that doesn't infringe on your marriage.

When you and your spouse discuss issues related to work, do you set aside time to do that, or do those comments emerge casually during dinner? Commit to separating your work discussions from your personal discussions with your spouse.

CELEBRATE EVEN THE SMALL WINS

Like any new habit, getting on the same page with your spouse regarding priorities and time together can take time. When you realize that you are working well together toward your shared vision, that creates reasons for you to celebrate. As you reach certain milestones, be sure to celebrate that success—even if it seems like a small one.

We believe people in general—not just entrepreneur couples—could benefit from stopping for a moment to celebrate even their small wins. You don't have to go on a month-long trip to Europe; a nice lunch or dinner together is enough. Or maybe just take time to get coffee together.

Those small celebrations keep you connected because you're both working together toward the same goals. And as you strive toward those goal and reach them together, it is empowering to encourage each other and the family.

We have learned to be intentional about celebrating even the small wins. For example, when Kay Lee completed her first Toastmasters speech, we went out for sushi. This is a goal of getting over the fear of public speaking. Even though she hasn't quite gotten over the fear, she made a significant first step. So that's worth celebrating.

Think about the past year or so. Did you and your spouse take time to celebrate even your small wins? Or did you rush on to the next priority? What are some wins you wish you had celebrated together? (Make plans to celebrate now.)

DON'T LET WORK INTERFERE WITH YOUR ABILITY TO HAVE FUN!

Our suggestions for getting on the same page have been pretty serious. But our final piece of advice is to have fun! When your entire life is focused on business and managing your priorities, it can seem like drudgery at times.

We encourage you to have fun together! That quality time that you are going to infuse into your relationship will do wonders for your personal and marital state of mind. Brainstorming your marriage vision together should be exhilarating and exciting. And as you reach even small milestones, celebrate in a fun way. Build fun into your lives. Make it a priority, and be intentional about it, just as you are intentional about setting aside quality time for each other.

I have to say, fun was not a hallmark of my corporate work experience.

One year, I was named the best sales performer at my company. I was ranked among the top 2 percent of all salespeople in the company's system. In fact, four salespeople from our district were named best performers, so our district itself was a top performer.

We each won an all-expenses-paid trip to the Grand Cayman Islands with our spouses, so of course I took Kay Lee with me.

Our first evening there, after dinner, the other winners, their spouses, and Kay Lee and I all gathered in the ballroom at our hotel. The vice president of the division got up and congratulated us for being top performers. He went on and on about our fantastic sales achievements. We were all basking in the praise and recognition.

But then, in the next breath, the VP said, "Now, while you are here this week celebrating, the rest of the sales force is out there selling. When you get back to the office, you'll be behind. So you're going to have to make that time up."

We all looked at each other, puzzled, as if to ask, "Did he really just say that?"

It was the first night of our top-performers' trip, and he was basically telling us we were losers.

So our advice is, when you celebrate your wins, don't let the pressures of work interfere with your fun. They're not going anywhere. When you celebrate, do so without distractions. And when you get back to work, you will work. But in the moment, celebrate your win.

As you know, that's just one of the many rewards we get as entrepreneurs. *We* set the tone for celebrating our wins! *We* make it a priority to encourage one another whenever possible.

What do you consider to be fun activities? What does your spouse consider fun? How can you build fun into your quality time together?

TANDEM BIKE CHECK

Scan the QR code shown below, or visit thetandembook.com/chapter-4, to watch a short video of us discussing this chapter. Also, you can download a free digital workbook that will help you create better balance in business and marriage.

Chapter 5

RESOLVE CONFLICT IN YOUR MARRIAGE AND BUSINESS

Conflict is healthy when you know how to resolve it.

"Peace is not the absence of conflict; it is the ability to handle it by peaceful means." | Ronald Reagan

Despite the many joys and benefits of marriage, it is inevitable that conflicts will arise. Every marriage counselor, therapist, and researcher will offer a different list of the most common sources of conflict in relationships, but there are common themes. A breakdown of communication, differing views about how to handle money, differing approaches to disciplining children, and unreasonable or unmet expectations are just a few of the top causes.

We often hear that most conflict results when a spouse misinterprets what the other one is saying. This falls into the "breakdown of communication" cause of conflict. Many times, we base what our spouse is saying on assumptions instead of facts.

We typically learn how to handle conflicts in the homes we grew up in, from our parents and others around us. Some people are skilled at resolving conflict, but most are not. And when two people get married, they follow the models they saw as kids. If those models are vastly different—maybe one spouse tiptoes around tension, and the other wants to discuss issues—they clash. They have distinctly different personalities, communicate differently, and interpret things differently.

Neither of us had good models of resolving conflict growing up, so it was inevitable that we would have challenges together. We don't blame our parents much because they just modeled what they learned. Very few people are trained in how to manage conflict, so it's no secret that most are, at best, mediocre at it. Even though my dad was a pastor, he didn't know how to resolve conflict well. You would think they would teach that in seminary, right?

In the end, the *cause* of a conflict is much less important than *resolving* it. Unresolved conflicts cause long-term damage. They erode trust and intimacy. And when you resolve conflicts by working through them as a couple, it brings you closer. You understand each other better. Plus, you have a funny story to reminisce about later! Too many people try to *avoid* conflicts. By doing so, they are missing out on healthy opportunities for discovering more about each other.

In this chapter, we dispel some myths about conflicts and offer practical strategies for resolving conflict. But first, Kay Lee and I want to share a conflict we experienced a few years back. Like many, it arose from a lack of clear communication. If it weren't for the conflict-resolution skills we learned in premarital counseling, it could have evolved into a serious argument.

THE GREEN CHILE STORY: A SIMPLE MISUNDERSTANDING

Here is a story that shows how a simple misunderstanding of one word can grow into a disagreement.

Almost daily, Kay Lee will ask me, "What do you want for dinner?"

Usually, I say, "I don't know."

That's not helpful to her, so we discussed it, and we made a deal. We agreed that Monday through Friday, Kay Lee will take the lead on the menu and cooking. On weekends, I will take the lead. We can help each other, and we can cook together, but the person who is taking the lead will decide what to prepare and then prepare it—be the chef, so to speak.

Now, even though Kay Lee takes the lead on weekdays, she stills ask me, "What do you want for dinner?"

And, as usual, I reply, "I don't know."

But one day, I was looking at the Allrecipes app, where we get a lot of recipes. I saw a recipe for green chile beef stew, and it looked really good. I walked into the kitchen and told Kay Lee, "Hey, I know what I want for dinner."

She asked me what it was, and I said, "Green chile beef stew."

She asked, "What makes the chili green?"

I said, "It comes green."

She said, "What do you mean it comes green? What makes the chili green?"

"That's how it's grown. It comes green."

Again, she asked me how the chili could be green.

One strategy we learned for conflict resolution during premarital counseling is to ask clarifying questions. So I asked her, "Honey, have you ever seen a green chile?"

She said no.

"What the…?" I'm saying to myself. Now I'm getting frustrated and a bit confused. "I know you've seen a green chile. We've cooked with green chile."

Then it finally dawned on me that we were talking about two different things. So I asked, "What do you think I'm talking about when I say 'green chile'?"

She said she was talking about chili beans, like the kind of beans firemen put in a pot of chili—but dyed green. This discussion happened in March, around St. Patrick's Day. People were talking about making beer green and cooking green cabbage. So she was thinking that we would somehow make chili beans green, with green food dye. I was talking about the vegetable—green chile—and she was talking about the dish.

This conflict basically stemmed from a misunderstanding. I said one thing, and she thought something different. And then we went back and forth.

This is the typical pattern for many conflicts. Both people become frustrated because they're both envisioning something different. You are trying to communicate, but you just aren't on the same page. This leads to the "cycle of insanity," as we call it. Both parties say the same things with the same results. Frustration results.

Hopefully, you can see in this funny example that once I stopped trying to communicate the same thing to Kay Lee and tried to understand what she was thinking, the issue quickly resolved. That one clarifying question of "What do you think I'm talking about?" instantly cleared the air. That turned out much better than if I had continued trying to convince her that she's seen a green *chile* when in her mind, she's never seen green *chili*.

Once I realized what was happening, I told Kay Lee, "The green chile in the recipe is the vegetable."

We laugh about this story now, but it could have been worse if we hadn't worked to resolve it.

Most arguments result when everyone is talking but no one is listening. Stop and listen. Think of a conflict you have had with your spouse. To what extent did you ask each other clarifying questions to find common ground? Thinking back on it, what questions could you have asked to resolve the conflict more fully and more quickly?

AVOIDING CONFLICT IS UNHEALTHY

Avoiding conflicts, or leaving them unresolved, isn't good for anyone. As individuals, we are all quite different. We have different backgrounds, beliefs, values, worldviews, preferences, likes, and dislikes. We will never agree on everything, so we have to learn how to share our lives with one another in a way that respects everyone.

We have mentioned Dr. John Gottman a few times in this book. The award-winning researcher on the topic of marital stability and divorce prediction has proven that 69 percent of problems in a relationship are *unsolvable*. These can include personality traits and long-standing issues around spending and saving money. He emphasizes the fact that couples must learn to manage conflict rather than try to avoid it or eliminate it.[32]

It's important to note that unsolvable problems like whether your spouse puts the toilet seat down or up is not usually the issue anyway. What we argue about, like the toilet seat, is mainly a symptom of the deeper issue that triggers the conflict. A spouse may feel disrespected or not loved because the other one constantly keeps the toilet seat up against their wishes.

In other words, most of our conflicts are not about the toilet seat. So it takes patience and understanding to get to the root of the matter and manage conflict.

It's not about the toilet seat.

Many couples avoid conflict because they lack conflict-resolution skills, and the conflict ends up creating animosity and anger. So they'll do anything to sweep it under the rug. Their solution is to avoid talking about the topic. They think they are helping their marriage by keeping the peace.

32 "Managing vs. Resolving Conflict in Relationships: The Blueprints for Success," Dr. Marni Feuerman, The Gottman Institute, November 9, 2017, https://www.gottman.com/blog/managing-vs-resolving-conflict-relationships-blueprints-success/

The problem with this approach is that issues, differences, and misunderstandings that don't get resolved will fester and cause resentment to build. When you continue sweeping things under the proverbial rug, the next thing you know, you have this huge pile of resentment. At some point, you have to deal with it. Sadly, when it all comes to a head, it's too late to repair the relationship.

We have worked with couples whose inability, or unwillingness, to resolve conflicts resulted in the erosion of their bond, to the point that they became, basically, roommates. Unresolved conflict erodes intimacy.

But when you are able to discuss your conflicts, listen to each other, understand each other better, and agree on ways to resolve your differences, it brings you closer together. There is priceless value when both spouses feel like they are being heard, understood, and valued. You feel more connected when you have actually resolved a conflict. And that stronger connection deepens and strengthens your relationship.

When a couple knows how to manage conflict well, there is nothing they can't do and accomplish—including working in tandem in business.

How similar are you and your spouse when it comes to handling conflict? Do one or both of you avoid conflict? How would it benefit your marriage—and your life—if you were to get professional help in resolving conflict?

DISPELLING THREE MYTHS ABOUT CONFLICT

Somewhere along the way, myths about conflict have become strongholds in our society. The following are three of many myths we want to dispel about conflict.

Myth #1: "If we don't talk about it, everything will be OK."

Refusing to discuss an area of conflict is like trying to cap a volcano. Years and years of pressure is going to build up in the form of resentment, and it will eventually blow up.

In many ways, our culture encourages us to avoid conflict. We toss around old adages that reinforce the myth that avoiding conflict, or winning a conflict, is the best way to handle opposing views.

For example, sometimes, when confronted with conflict, people say, "I will pick my battles." This means that, when they deem the topic important enough to them, they will dig in their heels and fight! Goodness, this is a marriage we're talking about, not a military battle!

When you fight the battle you picked, you want to *win* at all costs.

Richard Slatcher, the Gail M. Williamson Distinguished Professor of Psychology and the director of the University of Georgia's Close Relationships Laboratory, points out the lack of wisdom in this approach. He says, "We often have the instinct to try to win disagreements, and that's a mistake that many couples make. Instead, they should be arguing for the relationship to win."[33]

When both spouses set aside their desire to "win" and agree to do what's best for the relationship, they strengthen their bond.

Proverbs 16:32 says, "Better a patient person than a warrior, one with self-control than one who takes a city." Fight for your relationship, not for your own victory.

Another phrase we hear sometimes is, "Mama ain't happy, ain't nobody happy." We're not sure where this saying originated, but it's meant to be funny. It implies that we need to keep Mama happy, or there will be problems.

We agree that the woman in the household—the wife and mother—sets the tone of the household. But too many times, people just "go along to get along," letting the mom (or whoever is the most vocal person in the household) get her way.

Countless men have joked that the key to a happy marriage is just to nod and say, "Yes, Dear." This saying is meant to be funny, too, but it isn't.

When couples appease each other to keep the peace, over and over again, resentment builds up. They feel they are not being heard, and their true needs are not being met. It's possible to live with that disappointment for a while, but eventually, something gives. Their health deteriorates. They seek affirmation and affection with someone else, and infidelity may result. Their trust and intimacy erode to the point that the couple

33 "New Research Links Conflict Resolution, Long-Term Health," Hayley Major, University of Georgia, UGA Today, October 7, 2020, https://news.uga.edu/research-links-conflict-resolution-long-term-health/

ends up living as mere roommates. Eventually, many divorce. Some continue to exist in the same household while despising each other.

Simply by learning how to resolve conflicts, many couples could save, and enhance, their marriages.

Myth #2: Marriage is a compromise.

Having a healthy, mutually beneficial marriage does require a certain level of compromise for both spouses. However, we believe that saying "marriage is a compromise" takes the idea of "giving in" too far. It creates a mindset of *negotiation* instead of *resolution.*

When couples compromise, one or both spouses often still feel cheated, like they gave up and lost. They compromise to keep the peace, to keep Mama happy, to go along to get along. But true resolution is when both spouses feel like they have *won.* So we recommend that you focus on resolution, not compromise.

Myth #3: The discussion is all about the "what."

When conflicts arise, they appear to be about the tangible thing—the "what"—that is the subject of the couple's disagreement. But most of the time, conflicts go much deeper. This is why, when guiding clients through conflicts, Kay Lee and I always drill down deeper to discover the meaning behind the specific disagreement—the *why.*

The subject of finances is one that creates a lot of conflict in marriages. Many couples avoid discussing money, sometimes because doing so was taboo in their families of origin. Yet getting on the same page with your finances is vital to the success of your marriage.

Let's say a husband wants to buy a new sports car, and the wife is against it. They argue about it constantly, but the fact is, the issue goes much deeper than the question of purchasing the car; it has more to do with their differing beliefs about money.

It could be that the husband feels like he has worked hard and wants to be rewarded. Maybe when he was growing up, his family didn't have a lot of money, and he always dreamed of having a sports car, once he could afford it. And maybe his wife came from a home in which the parents stressed the importance of saving money for the future and for unexpected expenses. To her, spending $70,000 on a sports car is akin to stealing her future financial security because now they have a lot less money in the bank or in investments. She sees that sports car as a threat to their kids' college education, their new home, and their retirement. She values other things much more than a sports car.

This scenario demonstrates a common mistake couples often make—focusing on the *what*, when actually, the real issue is the *why*.

To resolve this conflict, we want to figure out how important this particular car is and how important it is for the husband to buy it right now. If both spouses can agree to save up for the car over time and purchase it in five or seven or ten years, they can fit it in with their other priorities and make it work. That is a potential solution so both spouses can feel like they are winning—they are getting what they want.

In every conflict, we need to know what is important to both spouses. This goes back to our earlier discussion about vision. Sitting down to discuss what your vision is for your marriage is a critical step in your marriage. That vision will guide every decision you make—financial and otherwise—throughout your marriage.

Working through issues like this, again, leads to a stronger bond. When you get to the heart of the issue—the *why*, not the *what*—then you can devise a plan that enables both parties to win. Working together toward that goal keeps you both focused on the vision and priorities you agreed to earlier. It keeps you on the same page, as we discussed in chapter 4.

Which myths about conflict have interfered with your ability to resolve conflicts with your spouse, and how?

LEARNING HOW TO RESOLVE CONFLICT WILL ALSO BENEFIT YOUR WORK LIFE

If Kay Lee and I were educators, we would advocate to have conflict resolution built into every curriculum. Imagine what we could accomplish as a society if people learned, from an early age, to discuss their differences, respect one another's opinions, find common ground, and resolve their conflicts. Lives would be saved, careers would be enhanced, families would stay together, and individuals would be happier and healthier.

When you learn how to resolve conflict, you will be able to improve every relationship you have—not just with your spouse, but also with your children, family members, neighbors and also in your work environment—with your business associates, employees, vendors.

In the American workplace, many employees feel undervalued, unappreciated, and unheard. This was true even before the COVID-19 pandemic, and now this sentiment is more prevalent than ever.

In 2021, an organization called Achievers, which operates an "Employee Success Platform," released its fourth annual Employee Engagement and Retention Report, Their research found 71 percent more employees were disengaged in 2021 than they were at the beginning of 2020, and 74 percent wished they received more recognition at work. Also, 52 percent of employees were planning to look for a new job, a significant 43 percent increase from 2020 and 2019.[34]

In many organizations, leaders fail to listen to employees. They don't solicit and act on feedback, they don't respond to concerns, or both. When that happens, employees feel like it's useless to voice their opinions because the bosses are going to do whatever they want. They feel like their input doesn't matter. They become disengaged, and they begin to seek work elsewhere.

The same dynamic applies to customers. If we do not solicit feedback from our customers, and strive to improve the customer experience, they feel undervalued, misunderstood, and unheard. If customers voice issues about products or service but the business owner ignores them, they feel like the business is only out to make money and doesn't really care about them, their opinions, or their satisfaction.

Have you ever voiced a complaint to a company, and someone contacted you about it, seemed genuinely concerned, and took action to make it up to you? It is empowering to feel valued, understood, and heard. Customers are more likely to remain loyal to your company when they feel valued.

---

34 "New Report: Half of Employees Plan to Leave Their Job This Year. Here's How Leaders Can Prevent Mass Turnover," Marcel Schwantes, Inc., March 29, 2021, https://www.inc.com/marcel-schwantes/report-employees-plan-leave-jobs-leadership-strategies.html

Many times, customers don't expect anything tangible when they complain about something. They just want someone in the business to acknowledge how they feel. They just want to vent. They want someone at the company to know that a product, service, or employee interaction left them feeling cheated. Simply *listening* to customers to find out what they want, need, and expect can lead to stronger relationships—just as it does in a marriage. Keeping the lines of communication open, and listening, can go a long way toward preventing conflict from happening in the first place.

As either an employee during past years, or as a business owner now, think of a situation in which you or someone else felt undervalued, misunderstood, and unheard. What could management have done to foster a more encouraging culture? What can you do now that will lead your own team members to feel valued?

STOP THE INSANITY CYCLE

Earlier, I mentioned the "insanity cycle." A quote that is often attributed to Albert Einstein is that "the definition of insanity is doing the same things over and over again and expecting a different result."

This happens when people engage in disagreements and arguments. Each party states his or her view over and over again, maybe in an increasingly louder voice, thinking that somehow, the other person will eventually come to their way of thinking. They might state their case in a slightly different way, but they're basically saying the same thing and expecting the situation to get resolved.

One area that causes mild tension for Kay Lee and me is when I am running late but fail to let her know. She is sitting at home, worrying about me and waiting to hear from me. As the minutes tick by, her worry turns into being upset.

Let's say Kay Lee tells me, "You never call me when you're running late."

And I respond, "You are so controlling. Why do you need to know everything I'm doing?"

Then she gets mad and responds, "I'm not controlling you. It would just be nice if you communicated with me."

Then I start feeling a little defensive, and I respond with, "I *do* communicate."

And on and on it goes.

Like many disagreements, this one starts out with a simple statement—"You never call me when you're running late"—that I perceive or interpret as an accusation. It triggers a defense mechanism in me. So I defend myself and then lob an accusation at her: "You are so controlling. Why do you have to know everything I'm doing?" Then that triggers a defense mechanism in her.

Then, instead of listening to each other, we are defending ourselves. This cycle could go on forever—defend and trigger, defend and trigger. It's kind of a "rinse and repeat."

We call this "the insanity cycle." We adapted the concept from a 2006 book titled *The DNA of Relationships for Couples.*

If things get intense enough in an argument, then the gloves come off, and couples escalate the accusations, drawing from arguments from the past that never got resolved. You get further and further away from the actual topic at hand, and none of it ever gets resolved.

This maddening, ever-repeating cycle can be prevented by learning a few practical strategies.

EIGHT STRATEGIES TO PREVENT CONFLICT

Again, conflict in some areas of your relationship is inevitable. But much conflict can be prevented, simply by knowing each other well and treating each other with respect. Here are eight ways to *prevent* conflict.

1. **Learn conflict-resolution skills from a specialist.** We recommend either taking a conflict-resolution course together or working with an experienced coach or counselor who can work with you to develop those skills.

If you didn't have a strong role model for conflict resolution when you were growing up, chances are, you will lack the skills to resolve conflicts effectively and leverage them for growth and learning. We don't know what we don't know, so in many cases, it is beneficial to seek outside help from a specialist. Not only does the specialist lead you to learn valuable skills; he or she will work with you both to *maintain* those skills as you face various milestones and situations in your lives.

Just as a mechanic repairs your engine and tunes it up to keep it running smoothly, and just as a medical team operates on you and then helps you stay healthy, an experienced, knowledgeable, compassionate coach or counselor can get you on the right track with your marriage and keep you there.

2. **Follow the 80/20 rule.** We believe that 80 percent of what we say to our spouse should be praise, and the other 20

percent should be gentle, respectful attention to areas that could use improvement or correction.

Some spouses are better at giving praise than others. Kay Lee is better at giving me praise than I am at praising her. This is going to be especially important for someone whose love language is "words of affirmation." That person wants and needs to hear praise. Watch the way you speak. Be gentle and instructive, not critical, when something bothers you. Praise at least five times more than you correct. This is true of nonverbal communication as well as your words. Your nonverbal cues can affect someone even more deeply than your words.

3. **Know your spouse's love language.** We discussed the five love languages earlier. Kay Lee jokes that she prefers all five. We all do, really, but we each have a primary love language. As we mentioned earlier, Kay Lee's primary love language is "quality time," and mine is "receiving gifts." We tend to give others what we would like to have ourselves. So if I'm not focused on it, I will give Kay Lee gifts because that's what I like. But her primary love language is "quality time," so that's what she appreciates from me most. Know what your spouse's love language is, and make it a point to shower your spouse with whatever that language entails.

4. **Know your spouse's personality type.** We have all our customers take the DiSC profile (again, D = dominance, I = influence, S = steadiness, and C = conscientiousness) because it is an incredibly helpful tool for recognizing strong personality traits. Knowing what your and your spouse's personality types are makes it much easier to communicate effectively and prevent conflict.

I am a high "C," focused on conscientiousness. I tend to be a perfectionist. I like things to be done a certain way, and I have to watch the way I speak because I know I can come across as negative. My dad was not a big communicator, and when he did communicate with me, it was usually to tell me about the things I did wrong, such as getting a low grade or missing a couple of free throws in a basketball game. Spouses often do the same thing, so we all need to keep the 80/20 rule in mind.

Another personality trait I have, as a "C," is that I process information quickly. If you ask me a question, I can analyze all the facts immediately and give you an answer. But Kay Lee is an "S," focused on steadiness. She needs time to process information before making a decision. If I demand an answer from her right away and get impatient, that is going to cause her to feel rushed, uncomfortable, and maybe upset and defensive. It creates conflict between us because she needs time to think about it. This is why understanding your and your spouse's personality and communication styles is crucial for preventing conflict.

In the DiSC profile, a high "D" is a person who is focused on dominance. They are highly driven and sometimes come across as a drill sergeant, maybe even a bully. They want something done *now*. Whether it's in business or marriage, they want a solution right now. If a strong "D" comes across a high "S" like Kay Lee, who needs time to process, a conflict is likely to arise. If the high "D" doesn't understand these differences in personality and communication styles, he or she can assume the high "S" is stubborn, lazy, or stupid because they need time to process. Knowing these differences can help defuse issues before they begin.

A great way to handle this situation is that when a high "D" asks a high "S" for an answer and expects it right now, the high "S" can respond by saying, "Let me think about this. I'll give you an answer by three o'clock this afternoon." That will satisfy the requester's need for an answer, and it will give the other person a chance to decide on an answer. Both parties feel like they have won.

5. **Express your appreciation often, and share what you love about your spouse.** This strategy is also along the lines of praise. Thank your partner often, even for something small, such as taking out the trash or cleaning up a spill. Of course, as responsible adults, we need to do those things without having to be asked or thanked, but express appreciation anyway. It's really a subtle way of reinforcing and rewarding good behavior.

We can never hear these compliments enough! We cannot assume that other people know what we're thinking. We can't read each other's minds. Kay Lee and I begin each of our weekly meetings by sharing what we love about each other. This is a simple act but goes a long way toward fostering closeness.

Most of us are quick to criticize others when they don't do what we think they should, but we are less forthcoming with praise when they do things well.

If Kay Lee constantly points out that I get home late without letting her know, and she never praises me for what I do well, she is focusing on what I'm *not* doing well. The only acknowledgement I'm getting from her is when I do something bad. So, guess what happens? I repeat the bad behavior—maybe without even realizing it—to get her attention.

As humans, we tend to repeat what is reinforced to us, whether or not we want them to do it. If you have kids, then you understand that when you tell them, "Don't touch the stove," they touch the stove. Why? Because our minds pick up only the action command, not the "do" or "don't." In this example, the child's mind only hears "...touch the stove." So it's best to tell kids what you *want* them to do, like "stay in the living room and play." Then reinforce it with simple praise and love.

6. **Overcommunicate.** Most of us err on the side of not communicating enough, or not communicating clearly. For that reason, strive to overcommunicate. Unless your partner says it's OK not to overcommunicate on certain issues, discuss issues more than you think is needed.

7. **Listen, and strive for understanding.** .ow we interpret information is based on *how* things are said, not *what* was said.

By listening fully, striving to understand, and then responding gently, we can prevent many conflicts. Proverbs 15:1 (NIV) says, "A gentle answer turns away wrath, but a harsh word stirs up anger." And Proverbs 15:18 (NIV) says, "A hot-tempered person stirs up conflict, but the one who is patient calms a quarrel."

8. **Know your spouse's dreams and hopes.** Now, if you have sat down together and created your vision as a couple, you already know what your spouse's dreams, hopes, and vision are for the future. But this is such an important topic for all of us that we recommend discussing it whenever you can. Bringing up the subject of what your spouse wants more than anything else stirs up excitement and inspiration. Sharing those moments further enhances your relationship.

Review the list of eight strategies for preventing conflict in your marriage. Which one will you try first with your spouse?

NINE WAYS TO RESOLVE CONFLICT

Taking the steps we just listed to *prevent* conflict should create more harmony in your marriage. But for those conflicts that cannot be prevented, here are nine ways to resolve conflict. Of course these rules of engagement will differ for each couple.

1. **Fight fair.** Before you can fight fair, you need to know, as we discussed, what your and your spouse's personality style, communication style, and love language are. When you know what tends to trigger or upset one another, you know how to avoid upsetting each other. Discuss only the issue at hand. Don't reach back twenty years and bring up something that happened then. And avoid throwing hurtful barbs at your spouse in the heat of the moment because you are angry.

2. **Create a safe place and time for discussions.** Interrupting your spouse in the middle of a ballgame on TV or dinner preparation isn't the best approach for discussing a potentially sensitive topic. The interruption itself can set a negative tone. When you have something to discuss it's best to ask for a time in which your spouse can give you their undivided attention. When there are other distractions while you're having an emotional conversation, it can only increase the emotions. Also, having these discussions in areas of the house that are not meant for intimacy. The living room, den, backyard, or garage can work well. Coffee shops are ideal, too.

Avoid having sensitive discussions at the dinner table. That's where my parents aired out their differences, and it cast a gloomy shadow over our meals and family time.

Avoid having these discussions in bed as well. Your bedroom needs to be a sanctuary, a place of peace and connection. If it becomes a place where heated discussions take place, then it's no longer a place that is safe or conducive to intimacy. When couples fight in bed, the result is often that one or both of them dreads going to bed at night. Whether consciously or subconsciously, we tend to avoid those unsafe places where negativity presides. Find a neutral spot that isn't connected to your sense of family or intimacy.

3. **Know yourself.** Most of us are quick to point out what others are doing wrong while ignoring, or minimizing, our own contributions to a conflict. As Matthew 7:3 (NIV) says, "Why do you look at the speck of sawdust in your brother's eye and pay no attention to the plank in your own eye?" It can be tough to know, and especially to admit, our own faults. But remember, each of us is a part of the problem *and* a part of the solution. A marriage is a partnership, and both spouses contribute to both sides of the equation. It's not about who's right or wrong; it's about resolving differences and coming to a shared understanding. In the middle of that cycle of insanity, either spouse can step up and begin the process of resolution.

4. **Know your spouse's past and what his or her "triggers" are.** The way we perceive the world is based, in large part, on our early experiences. When someone goes through a traumatic situation that caused a lot of fear, pain, worry, or other negative emotion, similar experiences he or she has later in life can cause memories of that situation to come flooding back.

Let's go back to our earlier discussion about how Kay Lee gets upset when I don't let her know I'm going to be late. For one thing, that is disrespectful to her because if she has worked hard to get a nice dinner on the table, and I come home long after it's ready, that makes her feel bad.

Now think about someone whose parents died in an auto accident when he or she was a kid. Maybe that person waited and waited for the parents to get home, but they never did. That evening, the police show up, and the kids are whisked off to Family Services or to stay with relatives. And they learn that their parents are never coming back. Now, fast-forward twenty years. That person is now married, and his or her spouse is an hour late getting home. That situation, which might seem insignificant to someone else, triggers memories for that person of his or her parents' death.

It is critical that we know about the experiences our spouse has been through so we can avoid those triggers. They are painful and traumatic.

Just take one minute to call or text your spouse and say, "Honey, I'm going to be half an hour late." That one simple communication can go a long way toward avoiding those painful triggers. When you know your spouse's story, it's easier to express empathy and understanding.

5. **Create rules of engagement.** This is a way of setting boundaries—deciding what is allowed, or "in bounds," and what is now allowed, or "out of bounds." For example, if your spouse had traumatic experiences in childhood as a result of being compared to siblings or classmates, you might decide together that comparisons are out of bounds.

One of our rules of engagement is that Kay Lee and I give each other "warning shots." If we need to bring up a topic we know might upset the other, then we will let each other know about it. Sometimes, Kay Lee says to me, "Please, honey, guard your heart. I have something I need to discuss with you. Is now a good time?" She doesn't want to catch me off-guard. Her "warning" cues me in to be ready. It gives me a second to catch my breath and prepare to listen.

For example, because she knows that it can trigger me to feel like she is coming across as controlling, she might give me a warning shot about this issue. She might say, "I'm not trying to be controlling, but would you do me a favor and call me if you're running late? That way I'll know when to have dinner ready for you." That warning shot defuses my trigger and lets me know what she needs from me. It is solution-based.

This is much more effective than if she were to say, "You never call me when you're running late." That's accusatory.

Also let your spouse know, when you discuss an issue, what you expect from him or her. If you just want your spouse to listen, empathize, and provide encouragement—but not to offer a potential solution—say so. If you do want guidance on a solution, state that as your expectation. This can avoid further conflicts if the spouse isn't sure what to offer, and what he or she does offer isn't what the other spouse was seeking. Maybe one of you just wants a hug.

When Kay Lee brings up an issue with me and says, "I need a solution to this," then I am focused on finding a solution, and that prevents me from feeling defensive. We go into problem-solving mode instead of defense mode. It helps you get in the right mindset.

And if she says, "I just want you to listen to what I have to say" or "I want to run an idea by you; I don't want a solution," I go into listening mode. I'm not trying to solve anything.

Often, when we offer potential solutions to our spouses—especially if that's not what they want—it can come across as though we're telling them what to do. That can be upsetting. This is why it's important to state up-front what type of support you want from your spouse. Now, if your spouse has said he or she doesn't want a solution, but something comes to mind that you think might help, ask his or permission to make a suggestion.

I am generalizing here, but many men like me immediately go into problem-solving mode, while many women like Kay Lee just want to be heard and understood. In some marriages, the roles are reversed, but you get the gist. So you can see how husbands and wives get into arguments quite a bit. We tend to start talking about a problem without stating what we need up-front. Do you need to be heard or to find a solution?

During these discussions, both spouses need to be prepared for the possibility that the other spouse will become upset and/or defensive. When we discuss sensitive topics, even if we are both trying to operate within our rules of engagement, we can unintentionally trigger or hurt one another. If that happens, remain calm. Step up and be the one who stops the insanity cycle. And give your spouse the benefit of the doubt.

6. **Consider anything that's important to your spouse to be important to you.** If something is important enough that your spouse brings it up, it should be important to you as well. Too many times, people minimize the spouse's feelings. We are a couple, and if it's about one of us, it's about both of us. Minimizing or invalidating your spouse's feelings is damaging. Again, consider that something probably triggered a negative memory. Even thought it might seem insignificant to you, it is significant to your spouses. Offer empathy so they know they've been heard and understood. Empathy is not about admitting right or wrong. It's about letting your spouse know that what he or she feels or thinks is important.

7. **Take time to cool off if you need to.** Sensitive discussions can be overwhelming. And depending on someone's personality type,

it can become too much to deal with. Again, communication is key. If you need a moment to think, process, and gain your composure, tell your spouse you love him or her but that you need a moment to cool off. Just say, "I'm going to take half an hour. When I get back, we'll talk about it."

This way, you have a game plan. You're not avoiding the discussion; you're just postponing it for thirty minutes. This cooling-off period can prevent couples from saying hurtful things they will regret later or doing something else that's "out of bounds." Be sure to honor that proposed timeline; don't leave your spouse waiting to finish the discussion.

8. **Ask the magic question: "What do you need from me?"** Earlier, I mentioned that it's good to state up-front what you need from your spouse so you will know whether to listen or offer a solution. But that doesn't always happen. So when you find yourself in the cycle of insanity and it doesn't seem like the conversation is going anywhere, pause. Then ask the magic question, "What do you need from me?" The reason it's magic is because it instantly causes your spouse to stop, think, and tell you whether he or she needs you to listen or offer a solution. One time, I asked this question of Kay Lee, and she said, "I need a hug." It instantly stopped the argument. We embraced lovingly instead of being angry at each other. Isn't gaining clarity a lot better than the endless cycle we often find ourselves in?

9. **Forgive each other.** If you say you've forgiven your spouse but you bring it the same topic again as ammunition in another argument, the issue is not resolved. True forgiveness comes when both spouses feel heard, understood, supported, and validated. When that happens, both spouses can surrender the

> issue, never to be brought up again. Simply put, if there are hurt feelings, then an apology is in order, as is forgiveness.

It can be difficult to ask for forgiveness. It also can be difficult to apologize. But we have to set aside our own egos and defenses and do what will restore harmony in our relationship. Most of us never set out to hurt our spouse, but sometimes, we do so unintentionally. When that happens, it is important for the spouse who feels hurt to speak up. It's also important for the other spouse to understand what he or she said or did and then apologize. Too often, spouses end up invalidating the hurt spouse's feelings in an effort to absolve themselves of wrongdoing.

Each of us feels what we feel! We need to understand that our spouses will feel emotions that we don't feel at times. It is not helpful to try to talk someone out of feeling a certain way, shaming them for feeling a certain way, or telling them, "You shouldn't feel that way." This will only make them more upset.

This is another area that holds much opportunity for learning and growing as a couple. Your spouse feels what he or she feels. Try to understand why. Then acknowledge it and then ask for forgiveness. Apologize for making them, with something you did or said, feel that way. When you both make this a habit, things will go much better. Remember you're on the same team. You have the same vision. These bumps in the road, these conflicts, will happen. But working through them is healthy—and necessary.

"What do you need from me?" is the magic question that can resolve your next argument. Review the list of nine strategies for

resolving conflict in your marriage. Which one will you try first with your spouse?

Kay Lee and I believe that if you can learn how to resolve conflict in your marriage, you can enhance your relationship significantly and even work together successfully. Don't feel like you have to do this alone. We are living proof that neutral, third-party coaching or counseling from an experienced specialist can provide great value in teaching couples how to work through their conflicts and resolve them. We strongly recommend seeking professional guidance in the area of conflict resolution. It will help you in every area of your life.

TANDEM BIKE CHECK

Scan the QR code shown below, or visit thetandembook.com/chapter-5, to watch a short video of us discussing this chapter. Also, you can download a free digital workbook that will help you create better balance in business and marriage.

Chapter 6

WORK SMARTER, NOT HARDER

Increase Your Return on Effort

"Focus on being productive instead of busy." | Tim Ferriss

When business isn't going so well or the owners are trying to grow it, the go-to strategy is often to put more time in. Work harder. We get busier and busier at work and spend less time with our spouse and family. *Voilà!* Lack of work–life balance. So the concept of working smarter, not harder, is to stop being busy and start being more productive. When you're more productive, you're accomplishing more within the same amount of time. You can't gain more time in the day, but you can increase the margin of it in your life and business.

This chapter will help you review the areas of your business in which you can work smarter, not harder. We discuss the topics of money margin and time margin more in chapters 7 and 8.

LET OTHERS DO THE WORK

Many business owners often resist getting help. Why is that? One reason is that it can be difficult for them to give up control of the things they've done from the very beginning. They're afraid other people won't do things the way they would—the "right" way! This isn't sustainable as your business grows, and it's not a work-smart approach.

One of our clients had a property-development business and had a really difficult time letting go of daily tasks. He was making the sales calls, doing the bids and invoicing, overseeing every job, and managing the laborers. In fact, there were many times when he would actually pick up a shovel and help move dirt! He had a great team in place, and they did good work. Even though he knew he could rely on them, he still felt the need to do a lot of the work his team was already equipped to do. OK, let's be honest—he was being a micro-manager! This wasn't good for anyone—him, his team members, or his family.

For months, we recommended that he take a step back on certain tasks in his job. He finally did, and soon, he began to relinquish control to his team members. A few months later, he confessed, "Things are getting done well—and faster." In fact, he discovered that the less involved he was, the better and faster things got done!

As business owners, we do not want to be micromanagers. It's hard to admit when we're trying to control every aspect of the business, though. Even this owner said, "Oh, I don't micromanage." I always chuckle when I hear an owner say this. Have you ever met a micromanager admit that he or she micromanages? Never. Well, actually a few times that has happened. But even when they admit they micromanage, they can't help themselves, and they still do it. Control can be a hard thing to let go. If we really want to work smarter, not harder, we have to take a good, had, honest look at ourselves and determine if we're trying to control tasks we should be delegating.

We know that, as the owner, you just want to make sure everything gets done correctly. After all, that business is your baby. You figure that if you do it yourself, it will get done correctly, and no one will have to do it over. This sounds like a logical argument, but by taking this approach, you end up doing more managing than you need to. This eats up valuable time you could spend on more profitable activities.

When you micromanage, you are basically telling your team members *you do not trust them*. That squelches morale. Hiring well and training well can take care of this issue, to a large extent. If you have a clear idea of the types of people you need working for you and what their tasks need to be, then you can hire people who are well suited for those roles. Then you can train them to perform those duties in the way you think is best.

They will probably do things a little differently than you would, but that's OK. What's important is that things get done right. People grow and thrive professionally when you give them the chance to put their own unique "spin" on their tasks.

Yes, people will make mistakes, but that's how we learn. When you're a micromanager, you will see every mistake because you are hovering over your team members. When you're looking for trouble, you're gonna find it! Don't look for it. Focus instead on outcomes.

Employees who feel they are being micromanaged find it incredibly frustrating. The highest form of respect you can give someone else is to recognize their talents and let them perform their jobs well. Steve Jobs, Apple's cofounder, said, "I hire people smarter than me and then get out of their way." That's a winning attitude.

We encourage you to take a step back. Build a staffing plan, write job descriptions, hire great people, train them well, and then start letting go. You will finally start to regain your work–marriage balance.

The dynamic is similar to parents letting their children learn on their own. If parents do everything for their children all the time, those young people will never learn how to solve problems effectively.

Let's say you have two children who are old enough to leave by themselves for a couple of hours. You go to your appointment and come back home to find that everything is still in good shape. But now, what if you had video cameras throughout your house, and you have an app on your phone to see what they were doing all day. Maybe they're being rambunctious, throwing pillows and racing around the house. When the time approaches that they're expecting you to return home, they will put everything back the way it was.

Those are things you probably don't want them to do, and if you know you're doing them, you will be focused on their actions, when all that really matters is that they are OK, and your house is still OK, when you return. Yes, it might drive you a little nuts. But when you come home and nothing's broken, everything's where it should be, and they've done the chores you asked them to complete, do you really care? Wouldn't you rather focus on more important things?

Micromanagers and perfectionists tend to get really uneasy when team members and family members do things differently than they do. At home, couples argue about which way to load the toilet paper in the holder! Does it really matter, as long as you have toilet paper?

Micromanager check: Can you let others do the work, or does it ease your mind if you do it yourself? Is it possible you are a micromanager? If you think you're not, would your team members agree? Would your spouse agree? Do a self-check in this area.

BRING IN SMART(ER) PEOPLE

As we've mentioned, entrepreneurs launch businesses because they love what they do, and they excel at it, whether it's cooking, repairing vehicles, or consulting. No one is an expert at every aspect of running a business. When an entrepreneur tries to wear every hat, he or she is bound to make mistakes, which creates inefficiencies and costs you money. If you make just one inefficiency in each department of your business, that can add up to some big issues.

For example, if you do not keep up with your bookkeeping, you won't know where your business stands financially—what your expenses are or how much money you're bringing in, if any. We are surprised by the number of clients with good-sized businesses who do not have any kind of bookkeeping system. When we begin working with them, we have to look at their tax returns to get an idea of how their businesses are doing financially.

In fact, a lot of their financial details are handwritten on yellow legal tablets. Without some sort of system—even off-the-shelf programs such as Quicken or QuickBooks—it's really hard to manage your business and know what areas you need to fix. You can correct a lot of business issues if you just know where the money's going. A reliable accounting system will track how much money you're spending in specific areas. That enables you to determine whether those expenditures are worth the investment.

Warning: If you're starting to do the eye roll as you read about bookkeeping and accounting, then this is an area you need to pay attention to.

Finances are the top area of the business that owners pay the least attention to, yet it is typically their biggest headache. Sales are low, profits are low, expenses are high, and cash flow is an issue. What do we do? Work harder and try to increase sales? No—that's not always the answer. In fact, you can increase your profits and improve cash flow without increasing sales. But to know how to do that, you need to have your financial books in order, sit down with a good financial analyst, and the pinpoint areas in your business where you can improve.

Many business owners resist seeking help, many times because of pride. Once we convince them of the value in hiring experts who excel in various areas of business management, it becomes easier for them to take that step toward reclaiming their time and personal lives.

If you aren't sure what kind of help you need, seek out the help of a reputable general-business consultant. Or start with getting a good accountant who specializes in financial analysis for businesses. Not all accountants are created equal. Most CPAs are good at doing taxes and general accounting but not necessarily business analysis.

Once your business begins growing more and you identify specific areas where you could use guidance, you might want to seek out advice from a technology, personnel, or marketing expert. Typically, those aspects of business that you enjoy the least are areas where you could use some outside expertise.

We all have strengths and weaknesses, so surround yourself with people who are strong in areas you are not. And then let them do their jobs.

BUILD A PLAN

Every business needs a *business plan*—a written document that states the purpose and objectives of the business, how it will achieve its goals, an analysis of the target market and any competitors, potential challenges and solutions, a sales and marketing strategy, an operations plan, and a financial plan. A well-thought-out business plan helps you clarify your vision for the business, keeps everyone on the same page (once you hire employees), and gives potential venture capitalists an idea of the potential revenue your business can generate.

Once you have written your business plan, it is important to review it regularly and update it as needed. Your needs will change over time, and fluctuations in the economy, the stock market, consumer trends and expectations, and other factors will require that you keep assessing your goals and objectives.

Most entrepreneurs have no formal business plan. Although recent data on the quantitative benefits of having a business plan are scarce, older studies show the payoff associated with putting in the time and effort to create this important road map for your business.

One study conducted by a software firm revealed that entrepreneurs who completed business plans were nearly twice as likely to successfully grow their businesses or obtain capital as those who didn't write a plan. Of those who completed a plan, 64 percent grew their businesses, 36 percent secured investment capital, and 36 percent secured a loan.[35]

We advise our clients to start their business plans by looking at a three-year strategy—what their business will look like in each of the next three years. What is their projection for growth? What types of staff and technology do they need to support that level of growth?

As your business grows, continue to *anticipate* what types of additional resources you will need to support that growth. That means you need to figure out the resources you will need *before* you need them—you need to stay one step ahead of the growth. This will help you avoid rushing to hire people, which can lead to poor hiring choices. Give yourself time to interview the best candidates several times, hire well, and train thoroughly. Yes, it takes time and costs money to do that, but *not* hiring and training well is even more costly.

Again, you can hire a part-time virtual assistant at first. As your business grows, you can expand that role to a full-time position. You can ramp up the hours for your salespeople and other staff members as well, over time.

A business plan is the compass for your company. The details can change, but the direction generally doesn't. Do you have a business plan? If so, how often do you review it? To what extent does it guide

35 "A Business Plan Doubles Your Chances for Success, Says a New Survey," Rieva Lesonsky, last updated January 20, 2016, Small Business Trends, https://smallbiztrends.com/2010/06/business-plan-success-twice-as-likely.html

your business decisions? What is your vision for the future of your business? How satisfied are you with where the business is now? Whether your vision is to expand the business or to keep it running while you step back a little, what do you need to do to accomplish that? If you do not have a business plan yet, develop one.

When we mention a business plan to our clients, sometimes they picture elaborate, complex, forty-page documents. Your business plan doesn't have to be long—in fact, you can create a one-page business plan that accomplishes everything it needs to.

SCALE YOUR BUSINESS

The most effective way to work smarter, not harder, is to position your business to *scale*. Of course entrepreneurs want their businesses to grow, but there is a big difference between *growing* and *scaling*.

In general, *growth* occurs when a company adds new resources such as staff, capital, or technology, and its revenue increases as a result. In contrast, *scaling* occurs when revenue increases *without* a substantial increase in resources. This is why scaling your business needs to be a top priority.

According to the Small Business Administration, scaling is about your business's *capacity* to grow and the extent to which your business systems, infrastructure, and team have the *capability* to accommodate growth. Scaling a business means setting the stage to enable and support growth in your company and having the ability to grow without being hampered.[36]

Streamlining processes is a key factor in scaling. As your company grows, it's important to have systems in place, and/or team members, to keep that growth from creating bottlenecks and delays in delivery to customers. Hard work by the owner suffices when you're just starting out, but if your business is to grow and scale, you need technology and other people to keep up with your growth. Again, even an off-the-shelf software program or a part-time staff member can help you manage this growth at first.

In essence, scaling our business increases your capacity to grow while taking the load off of the shoulders of the business owner.

Even if you don't want to *grow* your business, allowing it to *scale* will result in business that is much more efficient, profitable, and sustainable and that gives you your life—and your marriage—back.

What are your thoughts about growing and/or scaling your business? Have you ever considered how it could enhance your profitability and your marriage–work balance? Write down some ideas for ways to grow and/or scale your business. What resources and structure are needed for your business to grow without it requiring more time from you? If you're not sure where to start, hire a coach or consultant to guide you. Chances are, this is an investment that will pay off significantly.

36 "How to Scale a Business," Anita Campbell, SCORE, July 15, 2019, https://www.score.org/blog/how-scale-business

EVEN THE GOATS ARE COACHABLE

It would be difficult to find a professional athlete who has no coach. In professional sports, even the most accomplished athletes have multiple coaches to guide them in building on their strengths and compensating for their weaknesses.

Many fans, coaches, and players consider NFL quarterback Tom Brady The Greatest Of All Time (the GOAT). For the uninitiated, he has won the most Super Bowls (7), most career wins (243), most yards thrown (84,520), most career passing touchdowns (624), and most Super Bowl MVPs (5), to name a few of his accomplishments. And he's still playing (he retired briefly for a month).

Most of his accomplishments occurred during his nineteen-year tenure with the New England Patriots. Then, in a blockbuster move in 2020, he was traded to the Tampa Bay Buccaneers and subsequently led his new team to a Super Bowl win that next season.

Imagine you're the quarterback coach of the Tampa Bay Bucs, and you're about to inherit the GOAT. There would probably a mix of excitement and anxiety going through your mind. What are you supposed to teach a player who has accomplished everything there is to in the sport? How coachable would he be?

Well, we had the opportunity to ask Brady's QB coach, Clyde Christensen, that very question in episode 98 of our podcast, "Power Up Your Marriage and Business™." Now, Clyde has also coached Hall of Famer Peyton Manning, so he's no stranger to coaching talent.

This was his response as to how coachable Tom Brady is: "The best want to be coached."

That answer kind of took us aback. I expected to hear that successful people are very coachable. But to say they *want* to be coached took it to another level. In fact, coach Clyde went on to say that you can lose the respect of a guy like Tom Brady or Peyton Manning if you come to a meeting or practice unprepared…as a coach.

We all can benefit from the outside perspective, expertise, and guidance of a coach. If you want to be the GOAT, get a coach!

Whenever you find yourself struggling with an aspect of your business, or you notice some sort of change, that can be a cue to seek help in that area. Kay Lee and I are always aware of situations like this. Recently, we noticed a decline in listenership on our podcast, so we hired a specialist to audit our podcast. We paid him to analyze what we were doing and how we were doing it and to point us in the right direction.

We could have spent time trying to get to the bottom of it, but we are not experts in this area. So we hired someone who is an expert in this area. He does this type of analytics for a living, and he does it for a well-known brand name. He pinpointed areas where we could make some changes, and we executed them. That was much more efficient and effective use of our time than trying to do it all ourselves.

Also, although marketing is my specialty, I do not excel in all the tasks associated with marketing. I excel in developing and executing strategies, but we have a team of copywriters, graphic designers, and web designers to take care of those specialized tasks. I could design a landing page for a website, but it would take me much longer than it would take an expert. When I hire experts, these jobs get done faster and better, and they produce results, as opposed to me trying to figure it all out. Plus, I get to spend that time meeting with clients instead.

If you spend ten or twenty hours trying to solve an issue, that's valuable time you could be spending with your clients—or riding in tandem with your spouse. Plus, there is no guarantee you will be able to find the causes and solutions because that isn't an area in which you have experience and skills. We don't know what we don't know! Paying for a subject matter expert is not an expense but an investment into your time and business. It multiplies your time and increases your results.

Paying an expert to guide you in business areas in which you are weak will improve your financial performance. It's an investment, not an expense. What areas have you struggled with in your business? Get help in that area today. If you have not sought outside help, why haven't you? Consider the benefits to your business, personal health, and family if you were to get outside help in those areas. Identify an expert who can identify the causes and solutions. Then execute the recommendations he or she makes, and document your return on that investment.

Invest in your own growth, as well as that of your business. I am in a mastermind group, which is a peer-to-peer mentoring group, and Kay Lee is in a Toastmasters group to build her public-speaking skills. Getting help accelerates your personal and professional growth. And when you learn and grow, you are able to work smarter instead of harder.

The bottom line is that, as business owners, we can get a much higher return on our time investment if we do things the proper way, whether it's marketing, finance, or operations.

IF YOUR CAPACITY IS ALREADY MAXED OUT

Quite a few clients have told us, "We don't really want to grow our business because we can't handle the business we have now." That is not an ideal position for a business owner. It causes the business to stagnate, and it leads to stress for the owner and everyone else involved with the business. That is always a red flag to us. It's not that we think every business needs to grow; that's up to you. But if you are stressed with the business you do have, that's not a good sign. When your business has reached its capacity, you should be thriving, not striving or struggling.

Think about a restaurant. Its dining room can accommodate a certain number of guests, so the only way the business can grow, without increasing the size of the dining room, is to serve customers around the clock—24/7—if it isn't already. If the owners add on to their existing building or move to a bigger facility without significantly increasing expenses, they have now scaled the business and enabled it to grow. They can serve more customers.

Now they will need more staff members to serve those customers—cooks, servers, busboys, etc. But those labor costs are manageable based on demand. If most of their staff members were working part-time, now they can move them up to full-time positions.

Just as every business can grow, every business can scale, regardless of the industry, size, location, and other factors.

We have seen clients increase their marketing efforts, which results in more customers, but they do not have the capacity to accommodate those new customers. If you don't have the foundation in place to support your growth, your sales volume will outgrow your capacity to handle it. That can create stress and confusion. Orders can fall through the cracks.

There will be more inefficiency, mistakes, and miscommunication, which leads to unhappy customers and team members. The come the bad reviews online. You cannot afford that.

Remember this rule of thumb. One out of every ten happy customers will tell a friend. Every unhappy customer will tell ten people.

By running your business more efficiently—by growing and scaling it without having to put in more time at the office—you can achieve better work–marriage balance. It's about looking at the big picture and putting pieces into place for the business to be able to handle growth without exceeding your business's capacity to grow and handle more business.

THINK LIKE A FRANCHISOR

The largest franchises in the world have grown exponentially because they scaled their operations. As of November 2020, Subway had 22,275 franchises in the United States and more than 42,600 worldwide. McDonald's had 14,428 locations in this country and more than 36,000 restaurants worldwide. (However, McDonald's revenues were nearly twice those of Subway.)[37]

Both businesses started out with one location. They grew and scaled because their owners worked smart, not hard! They implemented repeatable processes, procedures, and systems that anyone could replicate in any location. If their founders had insisted on doing everything themselves, they never could have grown exponentially like they did.

37 "This Is the Fast-Food Chain with the Most Locations in America," Steven John, Eat This, Not That! November 7, 2020, https://www.eatthis.com/fast-food-chain-with-most-locations/

These mega-companies did not grow on the backs of the founders or CEOs. Those individuals did not work around the clock to expand the businesses. Instead, they developed a "business in a box" model—a franchise. They provided the blueprint that anyone with little or no experience in fast food can implement to build a successful business. Think like a franchisor!

That is a great position to be in—having your business grow and expand, even if you're not there! The business plan is not just for you but for others to follow. As you create the repeatable systems and process that will increase the efficiency of your business, it makes it easier for new hires to learn and managers to implement. Whether you have one location or ten thousand, there will be consistency in the operation without you having to micromanage the process.

One fun thing I do whenever we travel internationally is to try out a Big Mac. Whether we're in Japan, Israel, Mexico, or somewhere else, we can go into a McDonald's and have pretty much the same experience there that we would here at home. It's not because I crave their burgers (sorry, McDonald's). Instead, it's because I want to see how consistent their burgers taste around the world. You know what? Except for one country, so far, I've found that a Big Mac is a Big Mac, no matter where you go. That's a testament to their consistency and quality control.

Whether or not you want to expand your business, when you build it in such a way that you could franchise your brand, you're now working smarter, not harder. You will have a business that other people can manage and grow. And it's not only the franchisor who owns multiple locations. I know McDonald's franchisees who own more than ten locations themselves.

If you had to be away from your business for a day, a week, a month, or longer, how smoothly would it run without you there? To what extent do you have systems, procedures, and processes in place that document and detail the ideal way to handle the functions of your business? If your business could use improvement in this area, make it a priority so you can grow and scale the business while also freeing up more time to spend with your spouse and family.

TANDEM BIKE CHECK

Scan the QR code shown below, or visit thetandembook.com/chapter-6, to watch a short video of us discussing this chapter. Also, you can download a free digital workbook that will help you create better balance in business and marriage.

Chapter 7

INCREASE YOUR MONEY MARGIN

Focus on profits, not revenue.

"Profitability comes from loyalty, productivity, and having a character base from which to work." | Zig Ziglar

Most entrepreneurs run their businesses right on the edge of solvency, with little or no margin for the unexpected. This is common because, again, they excel in the services they provide but have never had any formal training in money management or stewardship. This leads to the number one reason we see for business failure: running out of money (poor cash flow). The second-most common reason we see for business failure is poor marketing.

It's this lack of margin that leads to the owner working harder.

The common mistake many businesses make when faced with low profits is to try to increase sales. They think that if they work harder to generate more volume, it will cure the lack of profits. That seems to make sense, but most commonly, working harder just leads to working harder. Profits may increase a little bit over time, but not in the same relationship with the time put in and the sales generated.

Business owners get overly focused on the top line (sales) when they should be focused on the bottom line (profits). What's left in the bank is more important that what comes in. And the greater the percentage (margin) of profits is in relation to total sales, the healthier the business is.

Most business owners seek out the help of an accountant or bookkeeper for financial assistance, but not all of them are equipped to help make important business decisions.-The typical accountant is more focused on data entry, balancing the books, and trying to minimize taxes. It takes specialized training like that of a CFO or controller to understand business strategies for increasing a business's profit margins.

Plus, even the best bookkeepers and accountants can make mistakes. And if you don't understand the numbers side of your business and don't want to deal with it, who's going to check the accountant's work? Unfortunately, this is why embezzlement is so common in the business world—business owners just relinquish their control of the money management without understanding it all themselves.

Now, you do not need to be an expert in finance, and we do not advise that you take over this role in your business. But you do need to know enough about your finances to recognize when something might be off. You also need to commit to reviewing your books on a regular basis. This isn't a task most business owners enjoy, but it is necessary if you are to increase your margin of money.

The key to making more money with fewer resources is to increase your margin. In terms of financial margin, this means giving yourself a little extra buffer in your budget, and a little more flexibility in your life, in general, to accommodate the unexpected.

In his book *Margin*, Charles Swenson, a medical doctor, describes the long-term damage we inflict on our minds, bodies, souls, and relationships when we live without margin. He also provides "prescriptions" for building more margin into every aspect of our lives. Here is how he compares a "marginless" approach to one that builds in more life-sustaining margin:[38]

> The conditions of modern-day living devour margin… Marginless is being thirty minutes late to the doctor's office because you were twenty minutes late getting out of the bank because you were ten minutes late dropping the kids off at school because the car ran out of gas two blocks from the gas station—and you forgot your wallet.
>
> Margin, on the other hand, is having breath left at the top of the staircase, money left at the end of the month, and sanity left at the end of adolescence.
>
> Marginless is fatigue; margin is energy. Marginless is red ink; margin is black ink. Margin is hurry; margin is calm…

One of the common denominators we see among solopreneurs and couplepreneurs is that they are living marginless lives, constantly driven to the edge of their limits, burning themselves out. After a while, they

38 Richard A. Swenson, MD, *Margin: Restoring Emotional, Physical, Financial, and Time Reserves to Overloaded Lives* (Colorado Springs: NavPress, 2004), 13.

have nothing left to give to their spouses and families because they have no energy left for even the most routine daily tasks in their businesses.

When business owners are working too hard, you can pretty much assume that they need to build more margin into their schedules and budgets.

INCREASE YOUR MONEY (PROFIT) MARGIN SO YOU CAN WORK LESS

We're going to be talking a lot about increasing profits in this chapter, but I don't want you think it's all about the money. Higher profits should not be the only goal for your business, although it's an important one for sure. The profits are what give you the ability to give raises and bonuses, save, and invest to build a better business—and in turn, your marriage.

Again, as we discussed earlier on the topic of scaling your business, your goal is to increase profitability without necessarily doing more work. Remember, *profit margin* is the percentage difference between your sales and your expenses. It has nothing to do with your *volume* of sales. It has to do with *the amount of profit after all expenses, including owners' wages, are subtracted as a percentage of net sales.* As a rule, we like to see a net profit margin of 15 percent of net sales.

The more you increase your money margin, the less you will have to work. Here is a simple example that you can see in the chart below. Let's say you have a product that costs you $1 each to make. You sell the item at two different prices at two different stores. One is priced at $2/unit and the other at $2.50/unit. This 25 percent difference between the low price and the high price results in a 50 percent difference in gross profit margin ($1.50 vs. $1.00). That means you would need to sell 50 percent more of the lower-priced product to make the same amount of profit.

The narrower your profit margin is, the more you have to work, and the more you have to sell. This is how you make more with less.

Also notice that the total sales volume and sales dollars are lower for the higher-cost item, but it earns the same amount of profit.

GROSS PROFIT					
Price	Cost	Margin	Volume	Total Sales	Total Gross
$2.50	$1.00	$1.50	100	$250.00	$150.00
$2.00	$1.00	$1.00	150	$300.00	$150.00

Increasing prices is the quickest and most efficient way to increase your profit margin. But because most business owners automatically assume that raising their prices will cause them to lose customers, they make the mistake of working harder to increase sales instead. We know what happens when they go down that path: the work load increases, it creates more stress on everyone, they start to burn out, and eventually, their marriages start to suffer.

In this example, notice the relationship between raising prices and increased profits. There is an exponential return of a 50 percent profit increase with a 25 percent rise in price. Or, to look at it another way, a sales discount of 20 percent (from $2.50 to $2.00) will force you to work 50 percent harder to earn the same amount of profit as before. That's why you need to be wary when you're offering a sale. Make sure you understand how much harder you need to work when you set a lower price or offer a discount.

One thought that may come to mind as you read this example is that those profit margins are much higher than the 15 percent goal I mentioned earlier. That's because in the example, I'm measuring *gross* profit margin, not *net* profit margin. *Gross* profit is the amount of money left after subtracting the cost of goods, which are the direct expenses associated with the production and delivery of a product or service. In general, managing price, cost of goods, and gross profit is how you can make the biggest impact on the net profit. After all, expenses and salaries are subtracted.

AVOID THESE FOUR COMMON PRICING MISTAKES

Pricing mistakes often result because business owners fail to consider the *value* of their products and services. They set their prices based on mathematical formulas. Let's look at four common pricing mistakes that leave value out of the equation.

1. **The "cost-plus" method**—That's when you mark up your cost of goods by a certain percentage.

2. **"Competitive analysis"**—That's when you look at your competitors in your industry and try to price what you're offering within their range of prices. You might have a superior product, but you find some feature about your competition that you feel is better than yours, so you price your offerings lower than theirs. Comparisons are dangerous because you inherently get caught up in measuring your weakness against your competitors' strengths. Most likely, there is something about your product or service that is better than most. Focus on that differentiating feature, and set your price accordingly.

3. **"Penetration pricing"**—That's when business owners set their prices a little lower than their competitors' in an effort to entice customers to try them out. Entrepreneurs often use this strategy when they are trying to break into a new market.

4. **A combination**—The fourth common pricing mistake is some

type of combination of all three.

The danger of these four pricing methods is that they are math formulas or arbitrary comparisons and assumptions that do not take into account the true value of your product or service. Yes, your costs and expenses are one factor to consider when setting your prices, but the *value* is even more important.

The reason most entrepreneurs don't price their offerings on value is because value is highly subjective. Everyone has a different idea and opinion about what something is worth, based on their own personal situation and perception. It's hard to put a number on attentive service, a pleasant atmosphere in a restaurant, expert advice, or a much-welcomed convenience when you're in a hurry.

Think about the way soft drinks are marketed in stores. You can buy a six-pack or twelve-pack of Coca-Cola from the shelf in the store for a few dollars. That makes the cost of each can 35 or 40 cents. You also can buy one can or bottle of Coke from the refrigerated case near the cashier. It might cost you $1.50 or close to $2.00 for that one can or bottle—that's a difference of more than $1.00 in the price of the same product in the same store. The price differential is convenience—being able to drink that cold Coke on your way home instead of waiting until you get back from the store to put it in a glass with ice.

Now, the value of convenience has an added cost to it. There are hidden labor costs associated with getting those single cans or bottles of soda into the refrigerated cases. Someone has to stock those refrigerators, which takes more time than setting one twelve-pack on a shelf. That store owner also needs to factor in the added cost of electricity to run those refrigerators. So the higher price is validated by the extra cost associated with convenience.

People who are focused on price would never buy that more expensive Coca-Cola in the refrigerated case! But there are plenty of people who are willing to pay more for that added convenience. They perceive value in the fact that the drink is cold. Convenience is more important to them than the cost.

Which of the four common pricing mistakes have you made? Assess the real value of what you are offering. To what extent do you make people's lives easier and solve problems for them? To what extent do your current prices reflect the value you provide?

VALUABLE PRICING ADVICE FROM MY MENTOR

Many business owners price their products and services a little lower than their competitors in an effort to gain more customers. This forces them to work a lot harder for smaller profits.

I made the same mistake when I started my consulting business. Because I was "new" to the consulting world, I felt I needed to charge less than more experienced consultants so I could gain clients in the beginning. This meant I had to work a lot harder to make the same amount of income than if I had charged double and served half as many clients. But who would pay me twice as much?

It was my mentor, Cam McConnell, author of *Build To Prosper* and the founder of MG LLC, who suggested I needed to charge twice my rate. When I gave him my reasoning for pricing lower, he asked me who I worked for. I told him about the previous Fortune 500 companies I had worked for. He then asked what they paid me for. I said, "Marketing and sales." Then he asked how much they paid me. I told him my salary, bonuses, and all the other benefits. H concluded, "If three Fortune 500 companies trust you enough to handle their marketing and sales while paying you handsomely for it, why shouldn't smaller, privately held businesses compensate you accordingly?"

In other words, he was saying, "Raise your prices, silly. You're worth it."

I did raise my prices as Cam suggested, and I immediately saw the benefit. Not only did my bottom line improve, but because I didn't have to stress and work so hard, I was able to pour myself into my clients and give them a higher level of service than I could have if I had been jumping from one client to another. It was a win–win. I had more margin of time and money and greater work–life balance.

Do a quick analysis of your work life. How narrow or wide is your current margin, in terms of money and time? What can you do to widen your margin, to give yourself some breathing room?

TARGET A HIGHER CALIBER OF CLIENTELE

To obtain five higher-paying clients vs. ten lower-paying clients like I did simply requires that you refocus on the types of clients you are targeting. First, set your higher rate and stick to it. Next, identify your ideal customer (target market) who is looking for your solution and will pay what it takes to solve their problem. Don't be afraid to say "no" to the ones who are looking for a deal. They tend to be the problem children. It's amazing—the customers who pay the higher price tag tend to trust you to deliver on your product or service and leave you alone, while the "let's make a deal" clients are emailing, texting, and calling you at all hours of the night.

For our consulting business, you might think our target customers are the owners of larger businesses earning eight figures or more. From a demographic point of view, that is true, for the most part. But from a psychographic point of view, our ideal customers are the business owners who want to have successful businesses *and* thriving marriages. They are frustrated that it's not happening and feel stuck.

Many of our clients have business revenue of less than $1 million per year. They're motivated enough for the solution that to them, our fees are worth it if we can help solve the problem.

From a target-market point of view, the psychographic of your ideal customer is more important to know than the demographic. The issue is not so much if they can afford what you offer; it's more about knowing if they are willing to pay for it. If customers value your product or service enough, they will find the money to pay for it.

We'll cover this pricing and margin issue in further detail in chapter 7. But we encourage you to consider this strategy. It can lead to a much smoother and more enjoyable tandem ride!

WHY BUSINESS OWNERS CHARGE TOO LITTLE

It seems like most small and medium-sized businesses charge too little. Even Fortune 500 companies, like one of the pharmaceutical companies I worked for, fall into the low-price trap. This topic is a marketing-related issue I am really passionate about because it makes a significant difference in business owners' ability to get paid what they are worth and to enjoy more work–marriage balance. Charging appropriately for the products and services enables them to work smarter instead of harder. It also enables them to stay in business longer and to thrive instead of just surviving.

When a business charges too little, it is reflected in low net profits. This is important because the profits are what allow the business to save for a rainy day (or two years of COVID), investing into better software or equipment, increasing wages, and/or hiring needed help.

This type of investment into the business makes it run more efficiently and takes the load off the owner.

Here are two main reasons business owners charge too little.

1. Fear

One reason business owners charge too little is fear. They are afraid that if they charge too much, they will lose customers. As we discussed, this isn't necessarily a bad thing.

This is a natural response but is one made from assumptions. Owners always seem to assume they are going to lose customers with a price increase with no facts to back that up. Most businesses never test the market to begin with when they set their prices to see what their market will pay. They just set the price and let it ride.

So the primary way we help our clients get over the fear is to show the financial projections and ask these questions: "How do you see yourself able to make a healthy profit at the current price and expenses?" and "How much volume is it going to take to get to that point, and how much work is it going to take?"

Once reality is staring them in the face, they realize they need to make a change. It doesn't mean the fear goes away immediately but it's a big first step. The next step is to counsel them that it's going to be OK and to show them the proper way to introduce a price increase. This is different for each business.

We were hand-holding one of our clients through a 15 percent price increase. As you can imagine, she was nervous. After a few weeks, she finally sent out the letters to her clients notifying them of the increase. The only thing that happened was that the checks came in—at the new price. The only response she received from a client was one who told her, "We were wondering when you were going to raise your prices."

Business owners tend to be more price-conscious than their customers. As long as you're providing value, customers will not mind paying what your product or service is worth.

2. Trying to Accommodate Everyone

The second primary reason business owners charge too little is they try to cast a wide net. As discussed earlier, when you cast a wide net, you're trying to be all things to all people. When you try to appeal to everyone, you get no one.

Think about it. Is there a shoe, restaurant, dress, phone, computer, couch, house, or car that appeals to everyone? No, because there are so many nuances to these products and variables in customers' taste that it's impossible for any of the items to appeal to everyone. Plus, no business has the capacity to supply everyone—not even Amazon.

This wide-net mindset also negatively effects your marketing message. When you are trying to appeal to everyone, your promotional message is going to be very generic. Would you buy a shoe that's promoted to everyone for all occasions? No, you want a shoe that meets a specific need like running or going out for a nice dinner. People want a product they know is perfect for their problem.

So the more targeted your marketing effort is, the greater is the likelihood that you will connect to customers.

Many times, marketers talk about identifying their target market by creating a demographic profile of their ideal customer. *Demographics* is a quantitative list of facts like income, age, location, education, and sex. While this can be important information, it is also limiting.

A better way of targeting your customer is to understand the *psychographics* of your audience. This is a qualitative measurement. It's a list of subjective measures like emotional state, desires, lifestyle, interests, genres, etc.

When you put the demographic and psychographic profile of your target market together, you get a more complete picture of who you should sell to and how you should craft your marketing message.

If we were to rely only on demographic information, we would be limiting our options. Based on what our consulting fees are, we would assume the married entrepreneur who produces $3 million/year or more in revenue would be our ideal target market. This is a general truth because that size of business has the budget to engage with us without breaking the bank.

However, our ideal client isn't necessarily motivated to pay us based on what their bank accounts shows. The psychographic profile of our ideal customer is an entrepreneur who is frustrated by the lack of work–life balance, struggling to get to the next level of business growth, has a lack of time to work *on* the business instead of *in* it, and just wants answers.

When you find properly motivated customers, price isn't so much the issue. They just want results. Of course, there are the highly price-conscious consumer out there as well. But you don't want to try to get their business if it undermines your profitability. There are more than enough properly motivated customers who will pay your value-based price. So go get them!

When you first set your prices, what method did you use? Now that you've read these recommendations, what would you do differently?

PRICE YOUR OFFERINGS BASED ON THEIR VALUE TO CUSTOMERS

We worked with a technology company that had three owners. To date, they had never turned a profit or paid themselves a salary as owners. They had a sales goal of $2.3 million in revenue to accomplish this.-But because their profit margin was so small, they could not achieve that goal unless they added another manufacturing shift to their schedule. And doing that would increase their labor cost.

Plus, to make an actual net profit of our recommended goal of 15 percent of net sales, they would have to reach total revenue of more than $3 million. This was going to be a huge reach because the owners hadn't even reached their first $1 million in revenue.

This is what happens when businesses set an arbitrary sales price without doing the financial projections to see what it's going to take to turn a profit. Unfortunately, this is very common. This is why we start with a complete financial assessment first. What we found in this case is the business did not have the current capacity to reach its sales goal without incurring higher expenses.

The primary mistake the owners made was implementing a penetration pricing model. They were relatively new to the industry, so they set a low price in an effort to cast a wide net, as many small businesses do. But without running a financial projection, they had no idea of the mountain they needed to climb.

After completing a financial assessment, we concluded they would need to increase their sales price by 86 percent! You should have seen the look on the faces in the room. It was a little like what you might be thinking right now: "What? There is no way our customers are going to pay that amount!"

When they expressed that doubt, I told them, "You're right. Not all of your customers will go for an 86 percent price increase. But the good news is, you don't need all of the customers. You just need the right ones. And as you can see, unless you find some significant way to lower your costs, you'll never turn a profit if you don't raise your prices."

This is a typical mistake many businesses make: trying to sell to all the customers. Casting a wide net. This mindset causes the business to arbitrarily set a lower price, which makes them work harder for little return.

Once we conducted an additional analysis of the business and quality of their product, it was clear they had a high value item that should be marketed to businesses, not consumers buying on Amazon. Businesses would be willing to pay the higher price for the quality they delivered. The typical Amazon customer is too price-conscious.

A few days after implementing the new sales price, a major corporation purchased not one, but five units of our client's product. This got the ball rolling for them to reach their first $1 million (actually $1.25 million) in revenue. And they achieved a net profit of 18 percent of net sales!

That's a big difference from trying to reach $3 million in revenue for the same profit margin.

You can either charge more and work less or charge less and work more. You decide. To what extent are you working harder than ever but not realizing your desired profit? Analyze your price point, or work with an expert to do so. Adjust as needed, even if it means you will lose some customers.

Besides achieving a profit, what did the higher price do for the business? It meant the owners didn't have to work like crazy people to fulfill demand. It also increased their margin of time, which allowed them to further increase the level of quality in their product and regain some personal time.

It's natural for an entrepreneur just launching a business to make assumptions about how to price their products and services, but they need to *validate* the assumptions on paper before actually going to market.

When running financial projections, most businesses will find they need to raise their prices. But you don't have to be afraid of charging higher prices. Like our case study shows, as long as the value is there, there are customers out there willing to pay the higher price. You just need to identify who they are and focus your marketing efforts on them.

DON'T BE AFRAID TO LOSE SOME CUSTOMERS

Now, the immediate fear business owners have when they raise prices is that they will lose customers—especially when raising the price by 86 percent! But I showed the tech-company owners how they could raise their prices by that amount, lose 75 percent of their customers, and still turn a healthy net profit of at least 15 percent, with a revenue goal of only $1.2 million, as opposed to $3 million.

That's quite a difference from not even breaking even and never getting paid a salary.

When they increased their gross profit margin—the difference between their sales and cost of goods—they made more money with less effort and fewer customers. They and their team members became less stressed, so they made fewer mistakes and were able to focus on the product instead of always chasing that break-even point.

This is one of the most common mistakes we see business owners make—keeping prices low so they can market to everybody, or casting a wide net. But when you set your price to match the value instead, it forces you to focus on who your ideal target market is. In the tech company's case, the owners discovered that their ideal target market was large corporations that buy multiple units of their product, not individual consumers who shop on Amazon and buy just one unit at a time. Corporations tend to be more concerned with quality than price, whereas many individuals often care more about price than quality.

It was a great fit—their ideal customers cared about quality, so the owners and their team members were able to begin focusing more on quality when they increased their price.

Now, most of the time, we do not have to recommend a price increase that high—86 percent was extreme. Most of the price increases we've recommended are in the range of 5 to 15 percent. Interestingly enough, when it's in that range, we often see an *increase* in customers, not a decrease.

Why? Because most consumers make value judgments based on price. Think about it. When an item is priced on the low end of the market, we assume it's of lower quality. On the reverse, when an item is priced on the higher end, we have greater expectation. So promoting high quality with a low price creates skepticism among consumers.

SERVE THE RIGHT CUSTOMERS, NOT ALL THE CUSTOMERS (TARGET MARKET)

If you ask a group of small-business owners who their target market is, at least half of them will say, "Everybody." But, as you can see, that is not a winning strategy because it forces you to price your product or service down to the affordability of the lowest common denominator. And that's when you end up working harder, with less money margin.

Regardless of how low you set your price, not everyone can afford it or will want it anyway. So it's a waste of time to try to market to everyone. And when you are offering a higher-quality product or service, the time, effort, and expense that go into it costs you more money. That is why comparison pricing is so dangerous. Many will set their price to be competitive against the competition without realizing that their expenses may be higher than their competitors'.

For example, Costco can sell a 72" Samsung LED TV for $400, while the mom and pop store down the street has to sell it at $650 to make a profit. How can the mom and pop store stay competitive? What if they were to price-match to stay competitive against Costco?

The answer is that the mom and pop shop would lose money if they tried to match Costco's price because Costco has economies of scale. The company sells such a high volume that it can purchase that same TV from the manufacturer for a lot less than most competitors. So price matching would cause the mom and pop store to lose money. This is what many businesses don't understand when they set their prices by comparing themselves against the market.

So, how *can* the mom and pop store compete against lower-priced competition?

The answer is by staying true to their value. In this case, the mom and pop store can compete against lower-priced competitors by focusing on customer service (value). They can have knowledgeable staff members available to help customers identify what type and size of TV would be best for their needs. A big TV is great, but what if it doesn't fit in the space allowed? Will they need help installing it on the wall, or is it best to set it on a stand? Will they need help setting up all the features, or will it be compatible with their existing audio equipment?

These are issues that a knowledgeable staff member could help the customer with. At Costco, good luck. Customer service is not their sweet spot. They offer a no-frills shopping experience. It's for people who know what they want and are interested in getting the best price.

Some consumers value price over service. Others value service over price. Instead of arbitrarily choosing who you want to target, identify what value you bring and the price you need to charge to be profitable. Then choose your target market.

When you target everyone, you reach no one. Narrow your focus on the audience you're trying to reach, and you'll have an easier time finding them.

AT LEAST KEEP UP WITH INFLATION

Inflation is always a factor to consider when pricing your products and services. If the previous section on pricing didn't convince you to increase your price, inflation should.

The annual inflation rate for the United States was 9.1 percent for the twelve months that ended in June 2022. That is the highest rate since November 1981, according to the US Labor Department.[39] On average, we see inflation of 2.5 to 3 percent per year. Inflation cuts into your profit, so be sure to factor this in when adjusting your prices over time. **If you don't** raise your prices for several years, you are losing profit without doing anything different. This is why it's typical for us to recommend a 5 to 15 percent price increase for our clients—they haven't raised prices for several years, they've lost margin, and they don't understand why.

INCREASE YOUR PROFIT MARGIN BY REDUCING COSTS WITHOUT CUTTING EXPENSES

There are three ways to increase your profit margin: increase price, lower costs, or both. It's a simple formula. The higher your price and the lower

39 "Current US Inflation Rates: 2000–2021," US Inflation Calculator, https://www.usinflationcalculator.com/inflation/current-inflation-rates

your cost, the bigger your margin. In our work with clients, we usually tackle it from both angles—we try to increase prices and lower costs.

To lower costs, you can seek out vendors who provide their products or services for a lower price than you are currently paying. You also can renegotiate contracts with vendors. Often, business owners think cutting costs means cutting expenses. That isn't always the best approach because when you cut expenses, you run the risk of lowering quality. You don't want to do that; instead, you want to make your business more efficient and increase your output without increasing the input. Here are two examples of ways to reduce costs by increasing output:

1. **Sell more per transaction**. The value meal in a fast-food restaurant is a great example of this concept. Left to their own devices, most customers would probably order a burger and a drink, without fries. But restaurants offer the value meal as an option, partly to make ordering easier for customers, and partly because it increases the value of each sale. The "value" in the value meal is that customers pay less if they order the entire three-item meal than if they were to order a burger, fries, and a drink separately. However, when restaurants advertise the value meals prominently, it makes the choice easier for customers, increases the odds they purchase three items instead of two, gives customers a discount, and increases the total sale and profit for that one order.

The value meals also "reduces" labor costs because it enables the cashier to key in all three items in less time than it takes to key in separate items. So it increases the output without increasing the input.

You may have noticed this "bundling' strategy with e-commerce companies. When you are shopping online and are ready to check out, sometimes a dialog box will pop up, enticing you to buy an extra item at a discount. The item really does cost less than the usual price, but if you add that item to your cart, the company has just increased the value of that sale.

How does this work for service providers like consultants, accountants, or gardeners? It's a similar concept. They can create bundled packages like a one-year bookkeeping package with tax-return filing or monthly gardening with twice-a-year lawn seeding. Like the value meal, the packages would have a discounted rate for the additional services, like tax-return preparation or lawn seeding, that encourage customers to buy the extra item they may not otherwise purchase.

2. **Increase efficiency**. Henry Ford revolutionized the auto industry[40] by innovating the assembly-line process. On December 1, 1913, Ford installed the first moving assembly line for the mass production of an entire automobile. His innovation reduced the time it took to build a chassis from more than 12 hours to one hour and 33 minutes.[41] Just imagine how much that saved the company over time—and enabled Ford to offer better prices than its competitors.

This increase in efficiency enabled Ford to increase productivity while also reducing costs—but he didn't reduce expenses. He actually increased his expenses, technically, by paying his employees twice as much to work shorter shifts. That created another impact as well: laborers wanted to work for Ford because of the higher pay, so Ford was able to hire the best workers. And that forced other auto manufacturers to raise their wages.

---

40 "Ford's Moving Assembly Line and $5 Workday," Corporate Ford, https://corporate.ford.com/articles/history/moving-assembly-line.html

41 "Ford's Assembly Line Starts Rolling," History.com, https://www.history.com/this-day-in-history/fords-assembly-line-starts-rolling

Now, let's review what increased output does for a business. In this case, Ford's production-line innovation increased output by 9x, which allowed him to increase wages by 2x while lowering prices to consumer by 3x. This benefited the company's bottom line, increased employees' bank accounts (across the industry), and allowed more people to afford an automobile.

Increasing efficiency can enable you to lower prices while increasing profits. How can you get creative and increase your output?

If you're a retailer, for example, an updated inventory system can automatically order inventory when it falls before a certain level. This reduces the chances that an item will be out of stock, causing you to lose a sales opportunity. It also makes the inventory and purchasing process quicker.

For consultant like us, we occasionally run mastermind groups to get valuable feedback from our clients. We meet with six to eight clients monthly to solve common problems, as opposed to meeting one-on-one. This allows us to drop the fees our clients pay significantly, while serving more people in less time and earning higher revenue in total. On the surface, it might seem like the clients get less value because our time is diluted among the group, but for the right customer, it is very beneficial. In a group setting, the clients form a community and encourage each other beyond simply solving business issues.

Think about the way your business creates products or services. How can you create more output in the same amount of time? Can you sell more per transaction? Can you increase efficiency? If so, how? Devise a strategy, and test it out.

Now that we've covered the topic of increasing your *money* margin, we will discuss how to increase your *time* margin in chapter 8.

TANDEM BIKE CHECK

Scan the QR code shown below, or visit thetandembook.com/chapter-7, to watch a short video of us discussing this chapter. Also, you can download a free digital workbook that will help you create better balance in business and marriage.

Plus! Bonus download:

4 Common Pricing Mistakes That Eat Profits eBook

Chapter 8

INCREASE YOUR TIME MARGIN

You can't create more time,
but you can create more margin.

"It's not always that we need to do more but rather that we need to focus on less." | Nathan Morris

If you are working harder than you'd like to, this chapter is for you!

In chapter 7, we discussed the importance of increasing your *money* margin to allow for unexpected expenses. It is just as important for you to increase your *time* margin so you're not always rushing, trying to fill multiple roles all at once, neglecting your personal life and marriage.

Time margin is the difference between the amount of time you have minus the time it takes to accomplish necessary activities. What's left over (margin) is the time you have to invest into the things that bring value to your marriage and business—the important activities that lead to growth. We want entrepreneurs to follow strategies for improving their margin of both *money and time* to achieve more marriage–work balance.

Operating with a narrow time margin is one of the most common issues we see among entrepreneurs. Entrepreneurs who lack marriage–work balance tend to operate within small margins of time. They rarely have time to invest to their relationships outside the office.

Not only is this stressful and physically taxing; it increases the likelihood of making mistakes, robs you of the joy of being a business owner, and eventually can damage your marriage. Because most entrepreneurs "wear many hats" and fulfill many roles in the course of doing business, they often spread ourselves too thin. Their team members do as well. But despite the frenetic pace of our daily busyness, most teams are not productive.

It's estimated that typical entrepreneurs spend 65 percent of their time working *in* the business—taking care of the daily responsibilities to keep it running—and only 35 percent working *on* the business—planning for future growth. We want to flip that ratio so you're spending 65 percent of your time *on* your business and only 35 percent of your time working *in* your business.

Again, we understand that most beginning business owners take care of all the daily activities—handling emails, phone calls, and responding to customer issues; billing and collections; preparing the services and/or products for customers; and working with vendors. Oh, and putting out "fires"!

That works for a while, but eventually, we need to evolve from that approach. We encourage our clients to prioritize hiring that first employee, even if that person works part time at first, so they can delegate some of those tasks to the assistant. This frees up their time to work on higher-revenue activities, as well as longer-term planning. Once you have someone else handling the details, you can focus on activities that can lead to growth, like doing research and development, conducting market research, making deals with big partners or clients, innovating, and concentrating on your vision and strategy. You are the only person who can handle those high-level tasks.

Some business owners have gained more margin in their schedules simply by investing in a software program. When you automate your processes, that streamlines some of your work, which saves time. For example, I use an automated calendar appointment system. When someone wants to make an appointment, with me, I simply send them a link to my calendar. They can find a date and time on my calendar that's open, and that also works for them, and then they can claim it and add their name, contact information, and reason for the call.

This is much more efficient than emailing back and forth, trying to find a date or time to meet. Just click and go! That strategy alone can save ten or fifteen minutes per scheduled appointment.

How much "margin" do you have in your time, relationships, and finances? In what areas would it help you to have more margin to allow for the unexpected? What practical strategies can you take to achieve that increase in margin?

WORKING HARDER ISN'T THE SOLUTION TO A LACK OF TIME MARGIN

To discover the areas in which there is imbalance, we ask our clients questions like, "What is working well in your business? What's not working well? How often are you able to take vacations, or at least weekend getaways, if ever?" Once we begin that discussion, people typically reveal the struggles and frustrations they are experiencing—often resulting from operating with narrow money and time margins. They will tell us, for example, that they are working every night and every weekend, missing their children's games and other events, feeling exhausted, experiencing health issues, and maybe arguing about time and money issues.

A review of our clients' financial statements typically reinforces our initial assessment about areas where they can work smarter, not harder—and regain balance in their marriage and work.

There is always a correlation between how much time business owners spend on productive vs. routine business activities and the extent to which they feel they have a good balance between marriage and work.

Time is not a commodity, as many refer to it. It is a valuable resource that is finite. Once it's gone, it's gone.

Unfortunately, the "default" for most business owners, when things aren't going as well as they would like, is to work harder. Put even *more* time into the business. Get more sales! Many times, they think, "If I get more sales, I will get more money, and then I can hire people to do work I don't want to do."

That is a natural inclination. But it never seems to happen. Depending on the company and its situation, generating more sales can create more stress instead of more profit. The solution Kay Lee and I recommend, instead, is to encourage business owners to *shift their mindset* and relinquish control of tasks they can delegate. It's always best to say "no" and/or delegate tasks that are not a good use of our time. Instead of trying to do everything mediocre, do fewer things with excellence. This will benefit your business and your customers.

Kay Lee and I were raised with a strong work ethic. This is an admirable trait; however, putting more hours into the business doesn't always translate to more success. Working smarter, or being more productive, is a better way of approaching the business. Greater productivity leads to increased output without having to give more input. Unfortunately for many of us, due to our upbringing, our go-to is work harder to get better results.

No one has ever taught most of us how to work smarter—or how to run a business. We just set out to offer clients our expertise and experience in a certain area, and we learn the rest as we go.

We wrote this book because we have learned much through the "growing pains" of those first few years of establishing our business and the issues that arose from our success. We hope you will learn from the strategies we provide here so you can learn how to work *smarter* without having to go through all that!

THE OBVIOUS ISSUES ARE USUALLY JUST THE BEGINNING

As we discover the underlying issues that are causing a business owner to work too hard, Kay Lee and I usually discover that those issues are just the tip of the iceberg regarding what's going on within the business.

If the owner is working really hard, the rest of the organization's staff members probably are, too. And if the owner is wearing multiple hats, his or her staff members probably are, too. When you combine the business owner's inefficiencies with the staff members' collective inefficiencies, it's easy to see how the entire organization can get bogged down with systems, processes, and mindsets that are counterproductive. Yes, all businesses have systems and processes. Most are organically created by the habits the company owners have developed. Unfortunately, they are not always good habits.

Many clients come to us for our marketing expertise, thinking more sales is the answer to the problems they are experiencing with their bottom line—or lack thereof. But as you hopefully are starting to realize, the real problem tends to be the variety of small inefficiencies that collectively add up to lower profits.

It's like the difference between a car driving on city streets versus the highway. A car goes farther on a tank of gas if it is driven strictly on a highway. The many starts and stops a car takes on city streets takes more energy and sucks up more fuel. This is like multitasking. Research shows that jumping from one task to another and back again takes more time than if you start and finish one task at a time sequentially.

Studies show that when our brains are constantly switching gears to bounce back and forth between tasks—especially when those tasks are complex and require our active attention—we become less efficient and more likely to make a mistake. One study showed that only 2.5 percent of people are able to multitask effectively.[42]

42 "Why Multitasking Doesn't Work," Cleveland Clinic, March 10, 2021, https://health.clevelandclinic.org/science-clear-multitasking-doesnt-work/

HIRE GREAT PEOPLE, TRAIN THEM, AND DELEGATE APPROPRIATE TASKS

We know from personal experience that when you are first launching your business, you do everything that needs to be done. You wear every "hat." You buy office supplies, handle the bookkeeping, hire and train staff members, work on your business plan, market your services, run to the post office and bank, and do *all* the customer work.

But as your business grows, there is no way you can continue to do that. There comes a time when you must delegate some tasks to someone else. Keep for yourself those tasks that only you can do or are best equipped to do.

When I first launched my consulting business, I was working on my website. It was time-consuming and tedious to keep it updated. I finally hired someone to handle that responsibility, along with some other marketing and administrative tasks. That freed up a lot of time for me to focus on the business, spend more time with Kay Lee, and have down time.

Not only did I have more free time, but the time I dedicated to work was revenue-generating. So the business grew because I spent less of my time on daily tasks. Earn more by doing less!

Many business owners are reluctant—and sometimes even unwilling—to delegate tasks that someone else could do. They are afraid that if they turn those responsibilities over to someone else, the job won't get done well. They have a hard time letting go! I'm a marketing consultant, but even I know I can't do all the marketing tasks. Plus, there are aspects of marketing that other people are better at than I am.

Trying to do everything yourself is not a sustainable mindset for long-term success. As your business grows from 5 to 15 to 150 people, you cannot—and should not—try to control every aspect of the business yourself. And, if you do try to do it all or micromanage, it limits the growth of your company. The key to making this work lies in hiring well, investing in training, and allowing people to discover their strengths and grow in their jobs.

Sometimes, a business owner will tell us, "I have this employee, but it's not working out."

Our follow-up question is, "Well, how much time did you spend training this person?"

Often, their answer is something like, "Oh, I don't have time for that. I just hired them and assumed they would figure it out." Or maybe they say, "Well, my brother needed a job, so I just put him in there."

Yes, it takes time, energy, and money to hire well and train well, but if you want your business to grow—and if you want to achieve marriage–work balance—it is essential to figure out which people you need to handle which tasks and what type of training they need.

But not all entrepreneurs are good teachers. They might be good leaders and innovative, visionary thinkers, but they are not always patient. In those cases, we recommend that they send an employee to train somewhere else or identify someone else within the company who is better equipped to train people.

In essence, the issues that result in marriage–work imbalance often stem from within the business. But that's where the solutions, are too! Once you begin operating more efficiently, building in more margin, streamlining processes, training staff members, and delegating tasks, you will probably find that your business begins to thrive more—and you begin to regain more balance between your marriage and work.

Are you holding on to tasks and responsibilities you could delegate to someone else? Do you require all your staff members to go through you for just about every decision regarding the business? To gain more margin, and more marriage–work balance, sit down and list the tasks that only you can handle and those tasks you could delegate to someone else. Then work on a hiring and training plan to get great people into those roles.

LEARN TO DELEGATE EFFECTIVELY

One of the most effective ways to increase the *margin* of time we give ourselves is to delegate tasks that are not the best use of our time. If you want to build a more profitable business without pushing yourself to your limit, you will need to delegate tasks to others. This is the only way you will have quality time to work *on* your business instead of *in* the business. It's also a key strategy for making your marriage more of a priority.

One of our clients had a capable team, but he resisted delegating more tasks to them because, as he reasoned, "It's faster if I just do it myself." He also reasoned that no one else could do the job as well as he could. As a result, he involved himself in the details of every area of the business. This prevented him from fulfilling his most important role—that of being the company's rainmaker. It was easy for *us* to see that if he would just delegate more work to his capable team, he could dedicate himself to growing the business. But *he* could not see that; it was his "blind spot."

A more effective use of his time and effort would be for him to *mentor* his team to grow professionally and personally. Not only would that strategy empower team members and inspire them to perform well; it also would remove some of the pressure from the business owner.

As is often the case, this entrepreneur didn't consider himself to be a micromanager—but obviously, he was! Most business owners don't recognize the extent of their unnecessary involvement in the daily business tasks as a problem until they begin to experience burnout. Finally, there comes a time when they are so exhausted that have no choice but to let others do the work. And then they wish they had "let go" much sooner!

A few months after he relinquished control of tasks he should not have been doing in the first place, he was finally able to get his more important work done. He said he felt a lot more relaxed, productive, and peaceful. In addition, his team members felt empowered once they saw that he finally trusted them to do their work on their own. Productivity increased, and everyone was happier.

THREE PRACTICAL STEPS TO INCREASE YOUR TIME MARGIN

Now that you know more about the concept of time margin and how it can make your life easier and more enjoyable, you can work to increase your own time margin. Here are three practical ways to do that.

1. Be aware that you're operating at the edge of your margins.

The first step toward increasing time margin is for you to simply *be aware* that you are operating at the very edge of your time margin. Many people are so accustomed to living "on the edge" that they aren't even aware that they're running themselves ragged. But self-awareness is a valuable characteristic for any business owner to have; it is a hallmark of effective leadership.

Some people can gain awareness about their own actions and attitudes that are blocking their growth. But more often, it's difficult for us to see our own shortcomings. Often, a spouse, family member, colleague, or consultant is the one who brings these issues to our attention.

2. Focus on the tasks only you can do.

Earlier, we said most business owners spend 65 percent of their time working *in* the business (doing daily tasks) and only 35 percent of their time working *on* the business (strategizing and building the business). Again, we like to see entrepreneurs switch those numbers around so they're working *on* their businesses two-thirds of the time. It makes more sense for you, and for the financial health of the business, to focus on your $100-per-hour or $300-per-hour work and to delegate the $20-per-hour work to someone else.

When you spend your time on lower-end work, you are losing money.

The reason most entrepreneurs spend two-thirds of their time doing busy work is because they are performing all or most of the roles in their businesses. They simply are not aware that they are not making optimum use of their time.

If this is true for you, you can turn the equation around simply by focusing on the tasks only *you* can do. Here's how.

A. Identify the top two or three tasks that would be the best use of your time—high-level, visionary, strategic tasks only you can do. These should be tasks you excel in, are passionate about, and enjoy the most—the work that inspired you to start your business in the first place.

B. Then, for at least a week, keep a log of the tasks you are doing and how much time you spend doing them. How much of that time did you spend on your most important high-level tasks? Not much, if you're like most business owners.

C. List the tasks you are spending time on that are not the best use of your time. Do this thoughtfully. Identify who is best suited to handle this work and would enjoy it and excel at it. Also notice which activities you're doing that are not in the best interest of the company at all. Maybe those are tasks you need to stop doing, either for now or forever.

D. Now create three lists of tasks: 1) The two to three growth activities you're best suited for, 2) tasks that someone else is better equipped to do that you will delegate and 3) tasks you will stop doing, either temporarily or forever.

E. Once you delegate and eliminate those tasks appropriately and settle into your new routine of working at a higher level, do another assessment. Log your time again, and see how close you are to spending 65 percent of your time *on* your business.

In the digital workbook you can download for free at the end of this chapter is a chart you can fill out for guidance in this area.

Now, your three lists of tasks—those you need to focus on, those you need to delegate, and those you will eliminate at least for now or forever—might change over time, depending on the growth stages of your business and other factors. In some cases, business owners need to focus on a different set of tasks just temporarily. Maybe they are going through a merger or having a new warehouse built, and those major endeavors require their attention until they're completed. So they have to say "No, for now" to the tasks they normally do daily.

Some tasks, like those in the "No, forever" bucket, should probably stay the same. QuickBooks is in Kay Lee's "No, forever" bucket, and running digital ads is in my "No, forever" bucket. These are examples of tasks that we probably should never do again, except for extreme emergencies. Avoiding them is not only better for productivity but for our mental and emotional state. Kay Lee gets in a bad mood when she manages QuickBooks. That's not good for our relationship.

One of our clients was really gifted at research and development for new products, so that is where it made sense for him to spend most of his time—he was a genius. But he consistently spent too much time on customer-facing issues. Not only was that a poor use of his time; his personality type was not ideal for that type of work anyway.

He was a little stubborn about changing his focus. Finally, after I threatened to lock him in a room without client access for a week, he saw the light. Now that he is focusing on R&D, he is much happier, and so are his clients! Plus, he is growing his tech company through new innovations and collaborations that only he can envision and develop.

Another client of ours was high on the dominance scale in the DiSC profile. She had a direct, rather abrupt way of interacting with her employees, and she demonstrated a lack of empathy for their situations. She was spending much of her time on tasks related to human resources—a task that needs to be in her "No, forever" bucket. That wasn't an ideal situation for anyone!

The solutions you use to delegate your work appropriately will depend on which "bucket" your less-ideal tasks are in. For example, if you need to stop doing training just for six months while you build a new office, you probably don't want to hire a permanent employee to do your training.

The best person to ask whether or not you're making good use of your time in the business is your spouse. They know you better than you know yourself.

3. Get some help.

Once you know which tasks are the best use of your time, you will probably find it a huge relief when you hire someone to help you in the areas you shouldn't be doing.

Today, you have more options than ever before for hiring support. There are more online platforms than ever that offer every kind of 1099 support imaginable, from virtual assistants to customer service reps to financial analysts and even chief marketing officers. You can hire them for 10 hours or 100 hours. Or you can delegate those tasks to team members who are already working with you, if they are well suited for those roles. If you have existing staff members who are interested in assuming some of those roles and seem like a good fit, you might want to invest in professional training for them.

Effective leaders and business owners ask for help in areas they are not strong in. This could mean working with a coach or consultant, hiring contractors, and/or training existing team members.

KNOW YOUR WEAK SPOTS, AND BUILD A TEAM AROUND YOU

Because most of our clients don't know their own weak spots, as we mentioned in chapter 3, we typically ask them to fill out a DiSC® profile, even if they think they know what their strengths and weaknesses are. Seeing the results of this personal assessment is extremely eye-opening; it makes business owners much more self-aware about their strengths and weaknesses.

As a reminder, DiSC is an acronym that stands for the four main personality profiles described in the DiSC model: (D)ominance, (i) nfluence, (S)teadiness, and (C)onscientiousness.

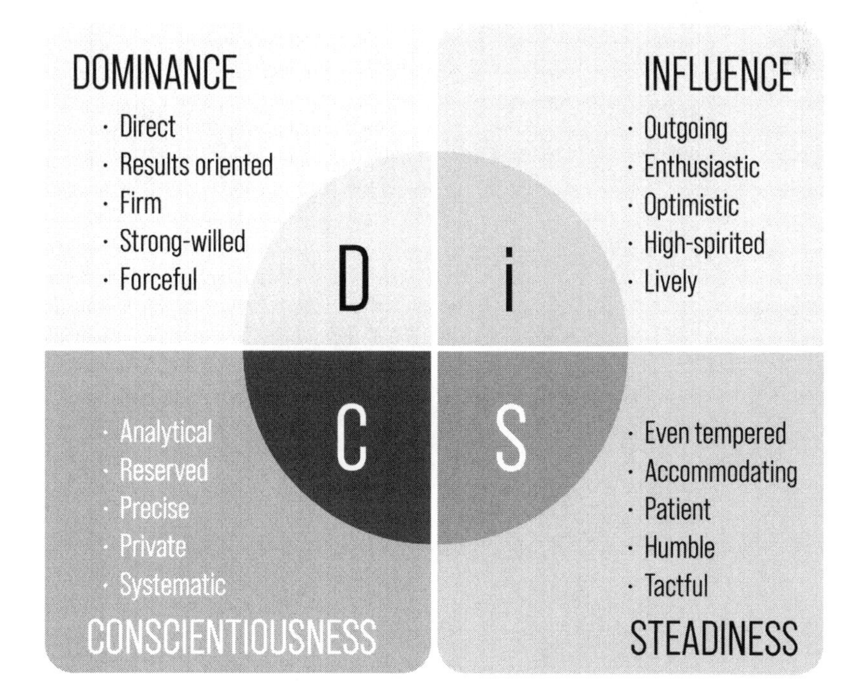

Each of the four personality types is characterized by strengths and weaknesses. Once we recognize our weaknesses, it's up to us to find ways to compensate for them. The following are some examples of leadership personalities and ways to complement their weaknesses with other people's strengths.

A HIGH D:
The hard-driving entrepreneur
EXAMPLE: ELON MUSK

Business owners whose assessments show they are high in *dominance* most likely have a "take no prisoners" approach to leadership. They tend to be direct, results-oriented, firm, strong-willed, and forceful. They're on the move because they just want to get things done This is a strength for them, but at the same time, it manifests in a way that isn't positive—people often think these high D's lack empathy and patience. It's easy to see how the high D's weaknesses could cause conflict in a business. They can come across as harsh, especially when people don't work as fast as the high-D boss expects them to. Instead of patiently teaching team members how to excel at tasks, they often just do things themselves. This isn't helpful to anyone.

To minimize the impact of these weaknesses tendency, high D's need to slow down, be patient, and let others do the talking. Also, it's typically better if they have someone else handle tasks that require patience, such as training and other personnel matters.

A HIGH I:

The life of the party whom everyone wants to be with

EXAMPLE: RICHARD BRANSON

Those entrepreneurs who are high on the *influence* scale are the "fun leaders" in a group. They are great at building camaraderie among team members and collaborating. They tend to be outgoing, enthusiastic, optimistic, high-spirited, and lively. They often make charismatic leaders who can influence people. Everybody likes them and feels inspired by them. But the downside of this personality type is that details often slip through the cracks.

Kay Lee is a high I. She likes to say, "I'm the fun one!" But as you can imagine, putting her in charge of QuickBooks is not the best idea. :-)

Many high I's are poor internal communicators as well. Often, they appear to communicate effectively with external groups—team members, partners, clients, and shareholders—but a lot of times, they're not good at communicating internally. Because they can lack attention to detail, they are often more focused on people than tasks. When they need something done, they can give vague instructions, leaving their team members with a lot more questions.

This is why high I's need to enlist the help of a skilled administrator or operations person to take care of details and internal communications.

A HIGH S:

The thoughtful collaborator who makes you feel important

EXAMPLE: LARRY PAGE, GOOGLE COFOUNDER

People who score high on the *steadiness* scale are considered the "nice" people. They tend to be even-tempered, accommodating, patient, humble, and thoughtful. They excel in supporting high D's and high I's. They can excel at interacting with others, but they often procrastinate and put off making important decisions because they don't want to "rock the boat" or make anyone mad. They tend to avoid conflict, so you aren't likely to see them letting team members know that mistakes have been made and need to be corrected. As a result, it's easy to take advantage of high S's.

To compensate for these weaknesses, high S's need to surround themselves with team members who drive them to take action and talk through issues with intention.

A HIGH C:

The analytical person with a high IQ

EXAMPLE: BILL GATES

And finally, business owners who score high on the *conscientiousness* scale tend to be analytical, reserved, precise, private, systematic, analytical, and sometimes perfectionistic. They do excellent, high-quality work but often work slowly because they want to double-check and triple-check everything. They can have a difficult time making decisions because they suffer from "paralysis analysis." They can't stop analyzing the data and weighing the pros against the cons. They also can be overly critical and prone to being micromanagers.

Because of these shortcomings, high C's need to delegate business tasks that require decisive and quick decision making.

I am a high C, so I can speak from my own personal experience. Thankfully, I'm well aware that sometimes I don't get things done because I'm constantly redoing tasks and triple-checking my work. I end up doing more work than necessary because I'm afraid that other people can't do something as well as I can. (Guilty as charged, and apologies to Kay Lee for all the times I've annoyed her in this way.)

Which DiSC profile do you relate with the most, and what can you do to overcome your negative tendencies? Everyone has strengths and weaknesses. What do you think is a weakness you exhibit in your business? How does it hinder efficiency or progress? What can you do to compensate for this weakness? If you hired a team member who excels in this area in which you do not excel, how would that help the business? How would it enhance your own quality of life and your marriage–work balance?

As you can see, all four personality types have amazing leadership traits but exhibit weaknesses that can prevent them from getting things done. This means we *all* can benefit from delegating certain tasks to other people whose personality types and skills complement our own. We all could benefit by putting more trust and faith in other people to take over tasks that they can handle more effectively than we can.

In his best-selling book *Good to Great: Why Some Companies Make the Leap...and Other Don't*, Jim Collins talks about "getting the right people in the right seats on the bus." Just as it's important for you to know your own strengths and weaknesses, it is critical for you to know the strengths and weaknesses of everyone on your team.

When you delegate tasks you are not good at and that are not the best use of your time, do it thoughtfully. Delegate them to people who might excel at those tasks and enjoy them. We see many inefficiencies in most teams because people are not "in the right seats." They are not working in roles that are a good match for their skills and interests. Now, this doesn't always mean you have to terminate people. Many times, a switch in roles increases productivity.

We see this in sports all the time. For example, there have been plenty of professional baseball and football players who started out in one position, but then the coach realized the player's talent would have more impact in another position. Maybe a coach brings a player onto the team to be a wide receiver. But over time, he sees that the player is fast but isn't great at catching the ball, so the coach reassigns him as a cornerback or a safety. Once that player is in the role that is best suited to his talent, everyone will benefit.

Similarly, in an office environment, let's say you hire someone in sales because he is outgoing and friendly, but it turns out that he is not good at closing sales. If that team member is a great worker, consider moving him over to customer service. It might be an ideal fit.

Just as we ask all our clients to take the DiSC profile, we recommend that you have everyone on your team take the DiSC profile. You will be amazed at how illuminating this exercise is. What you will learn about your team members' strengths and weaknesses (and your own) will enable you to structure your business in a way that leads to powerful interdependence. Everyone will be responsible for the tasks they are good at and enjoy.

Also, ask your team members what they do and do not enjoy. After assessing their skills and interviewing them to discover their interests, then figure out which tasks are best suited for each team member. When you take the time to discover your team members' true talents and interests, and then you build your team with those details in mind, it creates a more inviting culture with higher morale; greater productivity; happier, healthier team members who know you value them for their unique talents.

It is especially important for you to know what your spouse's talents and interests are if he or she is working with you in the business. All too often, we see business owners offload undesirable tasks onto their spouse, without considering what role he or she would excel in and enjoy. Please avoid putting your spouse in a role just because you have an "empty seat on the bus" and you need cheap labor! This is almost certain to cause resentment to build up, and it will damage your marriage and your business.

As the business owner, you are in a position of leadership. Great leaders encourage everyone around them to thrive by letting them make use of their unique talents. Great leaders also swallow their pride and reach out for help, knowing it will benefit them, their spouses, and their teams. Sometimes, the first step in asking for help is to reach out to a coach or consultant to determine how to improve time management and other aspects of business management.

Once you streamline who's doing what in your business, your productivity, morale, and quality of life are likely to soar. You will find that, finally, you are able to do more in less time. This, in turn, will enable you to devote more time to your spouse and marriage.

CONTINUE TO MONITOR PROGRESS

Once you have a good grasp on who should be doing what in your business, and once you have gotten the right team members in the right seats on "the bus," we urge you to continue to monitor your progress and make ongoing improvements.

At any time, for any reason, the dynamics in your business can change. It could be the result of a staff change, an economic shift, a new development in your industry, or something else. Just as it's important to monitor your financials and KPIs regularly, it's important to monitor your staffing and operations regularly. This will help you notice, and correct, any changes in morale or productivity right away.

TAILOR INCENTIVES AND REWARDS TO EACH TEAM MEMBER

Another benefit of knowing everyone around you well is that you can offer them incentives and rewards they are sure to appreciate.

Rewards, when used appropriately, can inspire team members to perform their best. People always appreciate commissions, raises, and bonuses, but you can make an even greater impact on team members by matching their rewards to their individual interests and passions. For example, some team members probably would appreciate time off from work more than a cash bonus. Others might appreciate an all-expenses-paid night on the town or vacation. You won't know this information unless you seek it out.

This concept is along the same lines as the five love languages we discussed earlier. When we know what other people enjoy, we can reward them in a way that truly makes them happy. In fact, Gary Chapman, the author of *The 5 Love Languages*, also wrote a version of that book for the workplace titled *The 5 Languages of Appreciation in the Workplace: Empowering Organizations by Encouraging People*. Following Chapman's advice can dramatically improve workplace relationships simply by learning your coworkers' language of appreciation.

Reward your team members based on what is meaningful to them. If you offer incentives, rewards, or gifts to your team members, to what extent do you personalize each one according to each individual's interests? Find out what they would prefer, either through the DiSC or other assessment, by discovering which "language of appreciation" characterizes them, or by asking them questions.

TANDEM BIKE CHECK

Scan the QR code shown below, or visit thetandembook.com/chapter-8, to watch a short video of us discussing this chapter. Also, you can download a free digital workbook that will help you create better balance in business and marriage.

Chapter 9

STOP SWINGING FOR THE FENCES

Small changes can lead to big outcomes.

"It is better to take many small steps in the right direction than to make a great leap forward, only to stumble backward." | Old Chinese Proverb

If you're a baseball fan, you know the saying, "Swing for the fences." It refers to batters swinging as hard as they can in an attempt to score a home run. We sometimes hear this phrase in investing as well, to mean that someone attempts to earn substantial returns in the stock market by making risky bets.

That might sound like a good strategy—to aim for the best possible outcome—but as we all know, despite our best efforts, hitting the ball out of the park in any endeavor is a challenge. In fact, Baseball Training World reports that only 12.1 percent of all hits made in Major League Baseball from the 2001 through the 2020 seasons were home runs.[43] This means that, no matter how talented the Major League players are, their batting average isn't high enough to warrant focusing just on hitting home runs. They are likely to be more successful by focusing on base hits and walks.

We believe this is true for business owners, too.

Many entrepreneurs are constantly looking for that one big thing that will propel the business forward—that viral video or slick marketing campaign that causes their phones to ring off the hook or the great review that drives thousands to their business. Now, those things can happen, but they're rare. So when business owners keep spending money to try to find that home run—that marketing "silver bullet" that will change the trajectory of the business—they often come up short and become frustrated. Like the baseball players who are swinging for the fences, they end up striking out more times than they hit a home run.

In this chapter, I'm going to walk you through an example of how we assess the various aspects of our clients' businesses to find the many small improvements that will lead to big results. *Warning:* These improvement may not be as fun as developing an amazing marketing campaign or creating market disruptive technology. However, they will make your business more efficient and profitable.

---

43 "What Percentage of Hits Are Home Runs in the MLB?" Baseball Training World, https://baseballtrainingworld.com/what-percentage-of-hits-are-home-runs-in-the-mlb/

Think of a time when you were "swinging for the fences" in your business instead of relying on a more measured, incremental path to success. How successful was your strategy? At what point, if ever, did you realize it made more sense to focus on a series of smaller successes?

START WITH THE FINANCIALS

If you hear the words "financial statement" and your mind draws a blank, you're ready to turn the page, your blood pressure rises, or you give an eye roll, then you absolutely need to pay attention to this section. I get it—the financials are not fun. They're tedious and boring. But they are the lifeblood of your company.

I hated accounting in college and did everything just to get by. Talking about credits and debits drove me nuts. Fast-forward to the present, and I find myself digging into financial statements all the time…and enjoying it. Why? Because that's where I find solutions to our clients' business dilemmas.

The first thing we do with every client is to look at the financial statements, profit and loss (P&L) statements, and balance sheets. The P&L statement is especially helpful in revealing gaps in the business and the factors that can help remedy them. As we've mentioned, financial details are the weak point for most business owners. Many lack experience or training with the financials, and they don't want to deal with this aspect of the business. They just want to perform the craft that is the basis for the business. They have their bookkeepers and accountants deal with the numbers.

I am a rather unusual marketing consultant because even though I am a marketer at heart, I'm concerned with the bottom line. Most marketers are focused solely on increasing sales. But you'd be surprised at how often increased sales results in lower profits. Yes, that can happen. One client spent so much in marketing (before retaining me as a consultant) that even though his sales grew 20 percent, he had a net loss in profits for the year.

Every decision you make has a financial implication on your business, either positive or negative. When you know how to monitor and interpret your financials, you can easily assess the health of the business before a problem gets out of control.

The financials that indicate the health of your business go far beyond just the bottom line—the net profit or loss. We also need to look at the cost of goods, fixed expenses, and the pricing strategy to see what's really going on.

Every aspect of your business is connected to a dollar sign. The time you and others spend working, every purchase you make, every ad you place, and every bill you pay—it's all connected to a dollar sign. There is a line item for everything you do. Those details are what reveal where the issues, and opportunities for improvement, lie. The real story is between your sales (the top line) and your net profit or loss (the bottom line). It's in the margins.

Now, knowing your financials well enough to know when a problem is arising is important. But you also need to know your key metrics, which we discuss next. By focusing on those two sets of numbers, you can identify any potential problem early and resolve it.

Money is the lifeblood of your business, so knowing how much you have and how it's being used is vital for your survival. How well can you read your financial statements and determine how well your company is doing? Get help with this, if necessary. You don't have to become a financial wizard, but it's important to be able to identify a potential problem before it becomes costly.

KNOW YOUR KEY PERFORMANCE INDICATORS

Key performance indicators (KPIs) are the critical (key) metrics that indicate your progress toward an intended result. They provide a focus for strategic and operational improvement, create an analytical basis for decision making, and help focus attention on what matters most.

Sales and profit goals may be your destination, but KPIs are the mileage markers along the way that help you determine your progress. The number of sales calls per day, dollars per transaction, clicks per email, and website views are all examples of KPIs.

For example, if you know it takes ten sales calls to earn one $1,000 sale, then you can establish a KPI to determine how many sales calls it will take to reach a sales goal of $100,000.

In this example, you would need to make 100 sales transactions to reach your sales goal. It would take 1,000 sales calls to achieve those 100 transactions. If you divide the 1,000 sales calls by 12 months, that equals 83.3 sales calls you would need to make per month. So establishing a KPI of 83.3 sales calls a month helps you understand how much of what type of activity will get you to your sales goal of $100,000.

Goal	Calls/$1,000	Total Calls Needed	Calls/Month
$100,000	10	1,000	83.3

These measures of progress vary by industry and by the aspect of business being measured. For example, you can track efficiency, effectiveness, quality, timeliness, governance, compliance, behaviors, economics, project performance, personnel performance, or resource utilization. The KPIs you establish should help you focus and measure the type of activity that will lead to the desired result.[44]

Many business owners don't know what the KPIs for their business are. And even those who *do* know what they are either don't focus on them or are inconsistent about monitoring and comparing these measures over time. As a result, business owners often don't realize they are losing money until their accountant is preparing their taxes and tells them, "You lost money." Knowing your numbers helps you take care of issues when they arise, before they get out of control.

As we mentioned in chapter 2, most business owners default to a focus on trying to get more sales when the business isn't doing well. Focusing on your KPIs is a much smarter way to get your business where you want it to be. When you see that a certain KPI is lower than you would like, you can employ strategies to improve it, a little at a time. As the tagline for this chapter notes, small changes can lead to big outcomes.

44 "What Is a Key Performance Indicator (KPI)?" KPI.org, https://kpi.org/KPI-Basics

KPIs are like a football team's statistics. Even if you don't know the number of wins and losses, you can determine the team's effectiveness by knowing how many fumbles and penalties the players incur. A winning strategy can be implemented by improving those KPIs.

EXAMPLES OF KPIs FOR MARKETING EFFORTS

Once you learn how important those measures of success, or KPIs are, you will be sure to assign a minimum metric for every goal you set, whether it's related to sales, employee retention, an investment in technology, or something else. You need to know the KPI for every business strategy—and then measure your business's performance in every category. That way, you know what is working and what isn't.

For example, let's say you decide to launch an email marketing campaign. How will you know if it's successful? One KPI to follow is called the "open rate." This is the percentage of people who actually open the email, not just see it in their inbox. An average open rate is 20 percent. But for a successful campaign, you may have a target rate of approximately 35 percent.

There are certain strategies you can use to increase that rate, and they vary according to the type of business. But one effective way to get more people to open your marketing email is to use a catchy, attention-getting headline in the subject line of your email. Finding just the right language to attract customers involves a lot of trial and error. A lot of marketers spend a lot of time trying to figure out the "secret sauce" that will improve their open rates.

Similarly, if you're doing social media marketing, the KPI you will measure is your "engagement level." That simply means the percentage of comments, likes, and shares your post generates in relation to the number of followers you have. The higher the ratio, the better your results. When you place Google ads, you want to measure the "click-through rate," which shows how many people clicked on the ad as a percentage of those who saw it. And if your ad is sending people to your site to sell a product, website sales conversions—the percentage of website visitors who make a purchase—is an important KPI to measure as well.

Whatever results you are generating from those marketing activities, increasing those percentages by a point here and a point there can lead to some bigger sales.

HOW IMPROVED MARGINS AND KPIs SAVED AN E-COMMERCE COMPANY

To illustrate how effective it is to focus on your KPIs instead of swinging for the fences, we want to share with you an inspiring success story about an e-commerce company we worked with recently that sells high-end men's fashion accessories. After hemorrhaging significant sums of money for years, this business became profitable once we got the owner focused on increasing profit margins, not sales. We increased those margins through properly established KPIs.

There were times when the company lost more than $1 million in a single year. Their best year came in 2019, when they ended the year with a net loss of $70,000. Then 2020 came around, and COVID hit. The resulting lockdowns hit this business especially hard. In November 2020, the business owners (three brothers) contacted us to see if we could help him turn the business around. At that point, they had experienced a net loss of $868,000 over the previous twelve months.

Tackling Five KPIs to Increase Gross Margins

My main goal was not to increase sales but rather to increase gross profit margins to 60 percent.

When attempting to turn around a business's profitability, there are many places you can begin. As we discussed in a previous chapter, price is the first place to start, but it's not always the only solution. You also need to look for areas in the business where you can reduce cost by increasing efficiency and production. For this business, we initially focused on improving gains in five general areas to increase the gross profit margin:

1. Improving product selection for wholesale customers
2. Increasing prices on select items
3. Increasing the average unit sales per transaction
4. Increasing website sales conversions
5. Increasing gross profit in the Amazon sales channel.

Let's look at each strategy in detail.

1. **Improving product selection for wholesale customers—** The company sold retail on its website and Amazon and sold wholesale to major department stores like Macy's and Nordstrom. As we assessed the financials, it became clear that the wholesale side of the business yielded more sales and the higher gross profit margins. So one of our first tasks was to audit the product selection the company was offering to wholesale customers on its website. We wanted to make sure

> the company was well stocked with items that were most in demand among wholesalers.

The VP of sales in charge of their wholesale sales channel was experienced. However, she often didn't have enough time to focus on product selection for the customer. So our directive to the leadership was to get her more help so she could focus on the activities that would drive sales.

That would increase profits. Promoting items that are not good sellers can be costly because there is a higher chance that customers will return those items. Processing and restocking returns costs money—especially in large quantities, as you have with wholesale customers.

In 2021, the average rate of returns of online purchases was 20.8 percent, according to the National Retail Federation. That's a jump from an average return rate of 10.6 percent in 2020. Shoppers tend to return goods to retailers at a higher rate when they buy online vs. in brick-and-mortar stores. Online sales accounted for roughly 23 percent of the $4.583 trillion of total US retail sales in 2021. Shoppers returned 16.6 percent of goods they purchased in stores in 2020, a jump from 10.6 percent in 2020.[45] Just making sure your wholesale customers have

45 "A More Than $761 Billion Dilemma: Retailers' Returns Jump as Online Sales Grow," Melissa Repko, CNBC, January 25, 2022, https://www.cnbc.com/2022/01/25/retailers-average-return-rate-jumps-to-16point6percent-as-online-sales-grow-.html?utm_source=Talking+Points+Newsletter&utm_campaign=18ac06039b-Talking_Points_September_22_2017_SafeHav9_22_2017_&utm_medium=email&utm_term=0_81a82d963f-18ac06039b-147017201&mc_cid=18ac06039b&mc_eid=3d7cd468a0#:~:text=Retail%20returns%20jumped%20to%20an,back%20at%20stores%20and%20warehouses

the right selection of items increases your profit margins because you minimize returns.

2. **Increasing prices on select items**—We assessed the company's pricing strategy to see if we needed to increase prices and if so, for which products. Since they had several hundred SKU's, we didn't go through each item to see if there was room for a price increase.

    - We looked at the top 20 percent of products that made up 80 percent of their sales and assessed their value as if it was for the first time. We considered material, craftsmanship, and unique design. But one key element of value for some of their products is their licensing approach. They are the only manufacturer in their fashion category that is authorized to use the likeness, names, and logos of some major professional sports leagues, teams, popular movies, and characters. They literally have no direct competition in this area, so those products can command a bit of a price hike. Instant profit increase!

3. **Increasing the average unit sales per transaction**—KPI = 1.2 units/transaction. We set out to increase the average unit sale per transaction—part of the profit strategy we discussed in chapter 7. The company's average transaction totaled a bit more than 1 item. So we started developing simple ways to increase the number of units sold per transaction—for example, creating two-item gift packages or installing a widget that recommends a complimentary item to their purchase at checkout.

    - If they were to reach a KPI goal of 1.2 units/transaction on their site, that would be a 20 percent increase in website sales.

4. **Increasing website sales conversions**—KPI = 1.25 average sales conversion. We set a KPI goal to increase the company's website sales conversions. Once a customer clicked on the website for any reason, they saw an average sales conversion rate of 0.8 percent. This means that for every 100 customers who visited the site, 0.8 made a purchase. We set out to achieve a 1.25 percent conversion rate (an average of 1.25 sales per 100 website visitors). Going from a conversion rate of 0.8 to 1.25 might not seem like much, but that's a 56 percent increase. This is an efficient way to increase revenue because you don't have to spend more to advertise on Google; you are simply converting more people who have already clicked on an ad to buy. This means a higher return on your marketing dollars as well, which increases both sales and profits.

5. **Increasing gross profit (GP) in the Amazon sales channel**—KPI = 50 percent GP. One of the biggest drags in profitability for the company was the GP derived from revenue incurred when selling on Amazon. It was a meager 34 percent when I started working with them. Because it represented a significant percentage of the overall revenue, increasing that GP to 50 percent would go a long way toward reaching the overall GP company goal of 60 percent.

The more complex a business is, the more moving parts it has, and the more areas there are for improvement. This business was relatively complex because it handled the manufacturing, marketing, and distribution functions for the wholesale and retail parts of the business. Each piece of the supply chain could be a business of its own. So there are many moving parts, which means there is more than one area of the business that can improve profits.

Remember, small changes can lead to big outcomes—especially if you make several different types of small changes at once. A review of the financials usually reveals that underperforming companies lag behind industry averages on many KPIs. We can achieve gains simply by increasing those averages.

Just as many business owners think the solution lies in making more sales, they often think the solution lies in spending more money on marketing. But many times, once I review their financials, I can see that they need to spend *less* money on marketing. Instead, they need to achieve a higher ROI on the marketing they are already doing.

PHENOMENAL RESULTS

With our focus on KPIs and small improvements in those five areas, the losses steadily decreased each month. And then, in September 2021, the company posted its first profitable month since they owned it. In November 2021—just one year into our work—the company posted an incredible 32 percent net profit. The business continued its progress, and as of March 2022, it had reached the "black" in terms of net ordinary income for the previous rolling twelve months. This is significant progress!

In my world, I'd rather outperform profit goals than sales goals any day.

I can't take all the credit, of course, because they had been making improvements in the business before engaging me as their consultant. But directing their attention to profit margins and establishing KPIs helped them focus on what drives the bottom line. And even though they failed to reach their sales goals, they outperformed their profit goals.

To show you how much businesses tend to prioritize sales over profits, when one of the owners told me the financial results, he mentioned how some of the team members were disappointed they didn't reach the sales numbers. I said, "Are you kidding me? Outperforming profit goals trumps sales any time. That's money in the bank. Make sure to tell them what a phenomenal job they did."

In this case study and most others, the lesson is that numbers might seem intimidating and confusing, but as a business owner, it is imperative for you to know your financials and KPIs. The old saying goes, "How do you eat an elephant? One bite at a time." This is true for increasing profitability in a business as well. Making a lot of small changes over time can result in a significant improvement in your bottom line.

Now, you don't have to learn how to do all this on your own. Hire a coach or consultant if you need to, but make it a priority to understand the numbers. Then you can monitor them and see how your business is doing at any given time.

These metrics are the key to your company's profitability, which, in turn, is the key to your ability to achieve more marriage–work balance.

Marriage–work balance is really the bottom-line indicator of how your business is doing in all areas, whether qualitative or quantitative. Your marriage and personal well-being will increase with each component of your business you improve. It's all connected, just like the two seats on a tandem bike.

TANDEM BIKE CHECK

Scan the QR code shown below, or visit thetandembook.com/chapter-9, to watch a short video of us discussing this chapter. Also, you can download a free digital workbook that will help you create better balance in business and marriage.

Chapter 10

STAY FOCUSED

Make sure you and your spouse are clear on the big picture.

"Everybody has a plan until they get punched in the face." | Mike Tyson

In the first nine chapters, we discussed quite a few strategies for improving your marriage and your business. Like any new skill, mastering these strategies will take time and practice. Getting your plan in place is the first important step; executing it well is critical.

And we know that not all plans work perfectly. Obstacles are always going to come up that you and your spouse will need to navigate. When something unexpected happens, as the Mike Tyson quote above states, it can throw you off. When that happens, you have to just get up and try again.

In this chapter, we reiterate some of the key strategies for achieving marriage–work balance, and we encourage you to stay focused on your plan of action. Don't let obstacles sidetrack you as you implement your plan. Eventually, you will notice improvements and begin to enjoy more balance.

Above all, make sure you're having fun during the process. Celebrate your accomplishments along the way.

BE PRESENT

Our lives get out of balance because we just let it happen. We come up with one excuse after another to explain why we don't have time to do date night, to share our hearts with our spouse, to play ball with the kids, and even have time to hang out with friends.

Yes, you're busy. We're all busy. But no matter how much time you say you don't have, you eventually do go home after work. You spend a certain amount of time at home. Make that time count.

When you're home, be present!

When your son or daughter wants to show you their latest doll or the fort they set up in the living room, pay attention. When your spouse wants to talk to you about their day or share something from their heart, put the phone down and listen.

One of our nephews told his mom once, "Listen to me with your eyes." That was his way of saying, "Put the phone down. I want to connect." I'll never forget that quote. Sometimes, kids are more tuned to what matters most in life than adults.

Listen with your eyes.

As you work to improve your business so you can have more time with your spouse and kids, make sure the time you do have with them is quality time. Five minutes of quality face-to-face time means a whole lot more than two hours of just sitting and watching TV or scrolling through Facebook.

BE RESILIENT

Sometimes, people come up with ideas that they are certain will rejuvenate their businesses, only to realize they weren't achievable after all. When this happens, you just have to rethink the strategy, determine why it didn't work, and correct it.

We can learn an important lesson about this from the Coca-Cola Company.

On April 23, 1985, the company announced that it was changing the formula for the world's most popular soft drink. It was the first time in ninety-nine years the company had changed its formula, and they called it "New Coke." Before unveiling the new version of the soda, they performed 190,000 blind taste tests on US and Canadian consumers. But they failed to ask those customers how they would feel if the company replaced the old version with the new one.

Customers didn't like the new formula at all. They staged protests and began to hoard the "old Coke." Some of the unhappy customers formed an organization they called "the Society for the Preservation of the Real Thing and Old Cola Drinkers of America. They claimed to have

100,000 members. After seventy-nine days, the company announced on July 11, 1985, that it was bringing back the original formula, and they renamed it "Coca-Cola Classic."[46]

An article on the company's own website acknowledges that this was "one of the most memorable marketing blunders of all time." The article admits that the leadership at the Coca-Cola Company was "swinging for the fences," as I discussed in chapter 9, in its effort to reenergize its brand and regain market share that was slowly slipping away.[47]

During the seventy-nine-day debacle, shares of Coca-Cola dropped on the New York Stock Exchange, while shares of Pepsi rose. But a few months after the Coca-Cola Company started selling the original formula again, branded as Coca-Cola Classic, the company returned to its position as the top-selling sugar cola, ahead of Pepsi.[48]

I think one of their biggest mistakes was offering the new formula and removing the old Coke from store shelves—they didn't give customers a choice about which version to buy. But after the company experienced the customer "rebellion," it offered both the old and new versions in stores.

They took a huge risk, and it did not pay off in the way they had hoped. However, once the dust settled, Coca-Cola dominated the market

---

46 "The Story of One of the Most Memorable Marketing Blunders Ever: The History of New Coke," The Coca-Cola Company website, date unknown, https://www.coca-colacompany.com/company/history/the-story-of-one-of-the-most-memorable-marketing-blunders-ever

47 Ibid.

48 "Why Coca-Cola's 'New Coke' Flopped," Christopher Klein, History.com, updated March 13, 2020, https://www.history.com/news/why-coca-cola-new-coke-flopped

again. This was a costly lesson, but it confirmed some important facts. For one thing, Coca-Cola's leadership realized just how loyal consumers were to its brand—not just consumers, but distributors as well.

Many of the distributors who sell Coca-Cola to stores are not owned by the company They are technically franchise operations and are typically independently owned. (How do I know this? Because my first sales job right out of college was with our local Coca-Cola distributor!) During that time, distributors objected to the switch in formulas, too, because it was hurting their sales and their relationships with the retailers who were *their* loyal customers. So it wasn't just strictly a business decision to reintroduce the original Coke; it was a decision based on relationships as well.

This is a great example of how even the best-thought-out plans don't always have the desired outcome. What's more important than having a plan not work out, though, is how you recover from a strategy that doesn't work out. The leaders at Coca-Cola admitted their blunder and brought back the version consumers wanted fairly quickly.

We can learn valuable lessons from this infamous situation. One such lesson is that the way you respond when things don't go according to your plan will help define your ultimate outcome. Another lesson is that you can't always base your decisions just on the business case; you also have to protect your most valuable relationships. In the end, your relationships are most important—especially the one with your spouse.

What do you think is a main takeaway from the Coca-Cola marketing misstep of 1985? What lessons, if any, from this historical marketing blunder can you apply to your business?

HONOR THE RULES OF ENGAGEMENT YOU AND YOUR SPOUSE HAVE CREATED

Because Kay Lee and I went through two years of counseling before we were married, we learned tools that we will continue to turn to throughout our lifetime to improve our marriage and business. The tools we've learned do help us prevent conflicts we might have otherwise, but disagreements still happen. The difference is that now, we are better at talking through our differences of opinion and resolving them without damaging our relationship. We've learned how to navigate the rough waters.

This is an important skill to have as you're maneuvering through your family and business plans. How you are both able to handle the road bumps along the way will determine how well you can achieve those big dreams.

Now, after sixteen years of marriage, Kay Lee and I understand, and honor, the "rules of engagement" in our relationship. We have learned how to avoid triggering each other...although there are still some tense moments! I realize I can be sarcastic at times, and when I make sarcastic comments to Kay Lee, they hurt her. They trigger negative emotions in her. I can still be sarcastic with the guys, but when I'm around Kay Lee, I have to leave my sarcasm at the door!

A somewhat funny situation comes up every once in a while when Kay Lee upsets me. As she mimics, I close my eyes, scrunch my face, make a fist with both hands and act as though I'm having a bowel movement. This is me trying to keep from saying something to her that I know won't go well.

She'll tell me, "Just say it."

I respond, "No" because it's not going to help the situation. It may make me feel better to release that sarcastic comment, but it will only wound Kay Lee. There's nothing to gain, and it's childish, so it's probably best to keep it to myself.

Like Momma used to say, "If you can't say anything nice, don't say it at all." Somehow in a marital conflict, we forget that simple but true statement.

But again, this doesn't mean we sweep our differences under the rug and avoid discussing them. It just means I need to cool off first and then discuss it with Kay Lee when I am in a better frame of mind.

If you agree with your spouse about everything, you are a unicorn! If you never have disagreements, it is likely that at least one of you is suppressing your true thoughts. We encourage you to improve your communication skills to the point where you both can express how you feel without prompting anger, judgment, or ridicule from the other spouse.

What types of communications do you and your spouse need to steer clear of, to avoid triggering each other?

BE COACHABLE

Often, spouses are insensitive without realizing it. An attempt to be funny can come across as an insult. (Guilty as charged!) I also believe people—especially men—are more coachable in the beginning of a relationship than they are later on.

This is why it is a good idea—and a valuable investment in your and your significant other's relationship—to go through counseling in the beginning of your relationship, or at least when things are peaceful. That's when you're still on your best behavior, showing your mate that you are willing to do what it takes to have a successful relationship. If you try to suggest counseling when things are bad, most likely, the other spouse won't want to go.

When your business is about to go bankrupt, or when a spouse has one foot out the door, on the way to speak to a divorce attorney, it can be difficult to repair what's broken. Sometimes, it's not possible to do so at all.

This ties in with one of our main themes in this book—again, get help when you need it, from experts who specialize in what you need to learn. Get coaching, counseling, or consulting sooner rather than later—before things are about to hit the fan! It is much easier to work out business and marital problems when things are still going pretty well. If you wait until it's a crisis, it can be more difficult to overcome.

In one of my first consulting jobs, I worked with a business owner whose company was about to go bankrupt. Neither he nor the team was very coachable. They had been in business for forty years. Every time I tried to introduce a new plan, strategy, or tactic, they would object, saying,

"No, we can't do that because that's not how we've done it for forty years." That was always their excuse—like a broken record (if you're old enough to remember that).

I would try to show them that the old way wasn't working anymore. I told them, "If you are going to avoid bankruptcy, things have to change. And before things can change, you've got to start doing some things differently."

They were caught up in the "insanity cycle" we discussed earlier, doing the same things over and over and hoping for different results. They were too comfortable in their misery to risk the change necessary to move the business forward. My advice is to be coachable, and ask for help as soon as a potential problem arises. It's not a sign of weakness to ask for help; it's a strength.

Remember, even the GOATs want to be coached. How coachable are you? How willing are you to let your spouse and other people offer advice and suggestions? If you are not as coachable as you could be, what is holding you back from seeking out helpful guidance from others?

LET'S FOLLOW OUR OWN ADVICE!

It's not uncommon for a coach to have a coach or for a therapist to have a therapist.

We have a client who is a marriage and family therapist. While we were introducing her to some exercises and strategies, she laughed and said, "This is what I recommend to my clients." But she admitted that it was sometimes hard for her to follow the advice she gives to others. I think that's true for most of us.

I am in a marketing mastermind group. The strategies the group recommends to me are often the same strategies I recommend to my own clients—but I haven't implemented them myself! I know I should be doing those things...but I just haven't.

It's similar to a medical condition; you will be more likely to heal or recover from an injury or illness if you get medical help sooner instead of waiting until it's too late. By seeing your doctor every six months or once a year to have a checkup, you are practicing prevention. We all need to work with experts who can help us correct any potential problems before they become unsolvable. Continue discussing matters with your spouse. Continue monitoring and evaluating your business. Address issues early! This helps everything continue to move in the right direction.

Three companies I've worked for in my career are all Fortune 500 companies. Everyone in those organizations, from the CEO all the way down to the sales team, would consistently evaluate their outcomes from the previous year to discover what worked well and what didn't. Then we would each build a plan of action for the new year. Constantly evaluating ourselves kept us focused on improvement.

But in small businesses, the entrepreneurs go year after year after year without evaluating what they are doing. They keep doing the same things. They might make some adjustments, but many times, they react to what's happening instead of being proactive about improving their outcomes. When business owners go five or ten years without assessing what's working and what's not, their businesses often erode, slowly, until small corrections aren't possible; their businesses need a total makeover.

None of us will ever be perfect, either in business or in our marriages. There is always room for us to improve. Recognizing the importance of constant evaluation is the first step in committing to ongoing improvement. Then make small improvements consistently. Remember, small changes can lead to big outcomes.

Don't wait until "tomorrow" to assess your business—start today. Sometimes tomorrow never comes. What types of advice do you offer to your clients or other people that you are not following yourself? What will it look like for you to begin following your own advice?

FOCUS ON THE BIG PICTURE

In chapter 4, we discussed how to "get on the same page" with your spouse. To do that, you have to know what you're building toward. Your one-page vision for your marriage that we recommend is a first step in accomplishing that. Keep the lines of communication open. Sit down and talk about the future with your spouse. Circumstances change, and they can change some elements of your vision. Discuss what the two of you want in your marriage and business, both for your immediate future and later—three, five, ten, or twenty years in the future and beyond.

Sometimes it's easier to figure out what you want if you start at the end and work backward. For example, you might discuss what your retirement will look like. According to Kay Lee, I will never retire, so I guess we don't even need to discuss that!

Imagine, and discuss, what your lives will look like when you are in your fifties, sixties, and seventies. If you are younger than that now, how will life be different for the two of you? What will change in your life? What will you need to change or adjust as you get older? What do you want to spend more time doing and less time doing? Once you have a clear picture of what you both want your lives to look like, then work backward. What needs to happen in your life and business to achieve those milestones?

Once you have identified your priorities together, support each other in accomplishing them. One of Kay Lee's goals is to become a successful public speaker, so she goes to Toastmasters meetings. I am not involved in those meetings, but to support her, I brainstorm ideas for speeches with her, and I listen to her practice her speeches and give her constructive feedback. Even though that is her goal, not mine, it will benefit our business. And it will benefit our relationship as we support and encourage each other. It's a detail, but it contributes to the bigger picture for us.

If you watch our videos, listen to our podcast, or see us on a stage near you (hopefully), make sure to comment to Kay Lee how well she is doing!

What will you do less of as you get older? We talked about the importance of delegating tasks to your team members. As you get older, you will likely need to delegate even more tasks.

What will your role in your business look like as you advance toward your life goals? What will change?

Let's say you're a mechanic, and you have done most of the work in your business. But looking to the next five, ten, or twenty years, you want to do less of the physically demanding work. Maybe you want to focus more on the administrative or the operational aspects of the business. Maybe you want to go out and talk with potential customers, strike partnership deals, or open another location. Write down a plan for the role you will play in those endeavors. Then list what you will need to delegate, and to whom.

Now, we're talking a lot about the future here. But it's important to enjoy life in the moment as you are planning for the future. Your dreams are like your finances—you need to have enough money available in "liquid" assets to access now, and you need money available in growth funds to support you in the future. Just like balancing work and marriage, we need to balance our future goals with our more immediate goals—in a way that satisfies both spouses' needs.

Kay Lee and I like to think of retirement as the beginning of an exciting new chapter, not the end of life as we once knew it. But we aren't waiting for retirement to enjoy life!

Dream about retirement together builds connection in our relationship. As with most couples, we each have some different dreams for the future. We enjoy discussing them and finding ways to bring our goals together in a way that's exciting for both of us. That keeps us motivated to keep working hard. It also keeps us on the same page. If one of us wants to invest in a property or buy a new car, but the other spouse wants to take the trip of a lifetime to Paris, we have to discuss all those options at length until we decide which goal we will pursue first. It takes communication and compromise! Too many couples avoid discussing finances, especially when they are *not* on the same page. This is not productive or healthy for a relationship.

We follow the same principle for shorter-term goals, such as vacations. We plan them well in advance. As we mentioned earlier, this enables us to save money together for those getaways, whether they are weekenders or longer vacations. Planning ahead also keeps us focused on sharing our future together, and we get to enjoy the anticipation of meaningful experiences together.

Just about all life goals have financial implications. Most of us have finite resources—and we all have a finite amount of time, of course—so we can't achieve all our dreams, at least not in the short term. One spouse can't expect to get every single one of his or her wants and desires met without also meeting the other spouse's wants and desires. The key is to determine what you are working for *together*.

Keep in mind that while it's important for both of you to get your needs met, you are a team, so you need to focus on your *collective* desires. To do that, one or both of you might have to postpone a dream until a later date. It doesn't mean you have to give up on it altogether. If you're not sure which option to choose, go back and read your marriage vision statement. Which option aligns best with what you both decided you want for the future?

You win when your spouse wins. Work as a team, and help each other reach your individual and collective goals. How well do you understand what your spouse wants out of life, and how well does he or she understand what your dreams and goals are? If you have not yet written a vision for your marriage, do so now. It will help you get and stay on the same page. Also, it will make it easier for you to work toward your common goals.

DEDICATE UNINTERRUPTED TIME TO DISCUSS AND PLAN ON AN ONGOING BASIS

Just as corporate teams meet regularly to discuss and plan what's going on in the business, couples need to do the same. This is why we recommend having regular weekly meetings together in the office—not at home. Your life plan is like your financial plan—you don't build then plan and then put it on a shelf. It's a dynamic tool that you will need to review and adjust often. It isn't likely that you and your spouses will have the same dreams at age seventy that you did at age thirty. Your life goals will probably shift over time.

If we're not paying attention, life can get away from us. We can get so caught up in dealing with what's right in front of us that we lose our focus on our future life goals. When this happens, we can become increasingly disconnected from one another because we're just two ships passing in the night. Having our regular weekly meetings over the past three years has helped Kay Lee and me a lot. It gives us dedicated time to discuss the business, and we make sure we both get to express what's on our minds.

Many couples just talk about the most pressing situations as they come up. This strategy doesn't create a consistent forum for open communication. Also, it can create conflict in a marriage because often, when one spouse wants to talk about a particular subject, the other one is not ready for it. Maybe they've got too much on their mind and are right in the middle of a complicated situation at work. It's just not the right time. Setting aside dedicated time to discuss things on a regular basis eases a lot of this tension.

During our weekly meetings, Kay Lee and I discuss what's going on currently. We also like to have a meeting once a month to discuss our longer-term plans and vision for our marriage and business. We even go on quarterly getaways, whether it's for a weekend or a long weekend.

Kay Lee and I used to go to a coffee shop for our business-and-life meetings. That got us away from distractions—the phone, the computer, etc. But during the pandemic, we weren't able to go out anymore, so I would bring coffee home for our meetings. Getting away from the place where you usually do business puts you in a different frame of mind and makes it easier to focus on the meeting. We have found that getting away from our regular routine makes our conversations more productive.

We do not discuss our work-and-life issues on date night! That is time we reserve simply for enjoying each other's company.

Every successful power couple we've met or interviewed has regular meetings. A great resource for scheduling your meetings is the Marriage Meetup planner from our good friends, Bill and Pam Farrel: www.love-wise.com/product/marriage-meet-ups.

REMEMBER...YOU'RE ON THE SAME TEAM!

There is no "i" in "team," but there is an "i" in "marriage." Yes, it is important for both spouses to be heard and to get their needs met. But whenever disagreements or arguments crop up—as they will—just remember that both of you are on the same team! Sometimes we get caught up in details that really don't matter in the bigger scheme of things. Yet we argue over them, and conflicts escalate that are difficult to resolve. If that happens regularly, that tension starts to erode the relationship.

When this happens, take a step back, remind each other that you're on the same team, and focus on the real issue. As the saying goes, "Don't sweat the small stuff."

I think it's interesting that when two people are dating, they are attracted by their differences. But once they get married, the very thing that attracted one spouse can become a source of irritation. We have to learn how to appreciate—and accept—each other's differences and strengths.

Sometimes, when Kay Lee and I get into a little tiff, I will ask her, "Do you really want to argue about this?" She will think about it for a second, almost get the face I get when I'm holding something back, think "Yes, it's a stupid issue," say no, and then we will regroup. Usually, it's something insignificant, and it's not worth fighting over. In fact, we never remember what the issue was.

GIVE YOURSELF GRACE

Even the most educated, intelligent, competent, experienced people stumble at times. When you do stumble, give yourself grace. Use the strategies in this book to resolve conflict, keep the lines of communication open, ask clarifying questions, step away to cool off if you need to, give each other the benefit of the doubt, remember your collective vision, and more. And try to recover gracefully, like the Coca-Cola executives did in 1985!

Your spouse will stumble, too, so give him or her grace when it happens. Have each other's back because remember, you're a team, and you are striving for the same great outcomes. You are stronger together than you are as individuals.

When I launched our consulting business, it started out well, and the first few months were going great. Then, all of a sudden, the business flattened out, and I wasn't getting any clients. I was doing everything I needed to do, marketing-wise, to try to get clients. But nothing was working. And then one day, it hit me that instead of trying to cast a wide net, like a lot of people do in marketing, I needed to focus on a few important relationships I already had in my network and dig deeper into them. It turned out that I already had everything I needed. I didn't need to expand my network to get more clients.

I kind of beat myself up because I didn't realize that sooner—after all, I had twenty-five years of marketing experience at that point! But I gave myself grace. I was just starting out in the consulting business, and of course there is always a learning curve with any new endeavor.

When you reach a plateau or stalemate, don't beat yourself up or let depression or discouragement take over. Just take a step back and take an objective look at everything. Ask yourself—and your spouse—"What am I doing wrong? How should I adjust? How can I fix it?" Something isn't working. What is it? Again, in some cases, it helps to have a third party help you analyze your operation and suggest adjustments.

Even the best make mistakes. Dave Ramsey and Walt Disney are just two of the many millionaires who have gone bankrupt yet recovered. Mistakes aren't the end of the world. Give yourself grace.

AIM FOR EXCELLENCE, NOT PERFECTION

Perfection is never attainable, so let's focus on excellence instead. This point goes hand-in-hand with the previous reminder to give yourself grace. Again, we are not perfect, and neither are our spouses. Still, it's easier to blame someone else when something goes wrong than it is to accept responsibility for our part in it. We need to take accountability for our actions. Remember, as a married couple, we are both part of the problem, and we are both part of the solution!

The next time something goes a little bit wrong, and you and your spouse are arguing about it, take a step back. Listen to the way you are talking to each other. Avoid saying things to each other like, "I wish you would do this differently" or "Why don't you ever do this?"

As Kay Lee and I know, that kind of language sounds accusatory, and it causes the other spouse to become defensive. We can get the same point across by rewording those comments as, "It would mean a lot to me if you would..." or "It hurts my feeling when you..." Reframing the statement changes the tone from making an accusation to asking for help.

Know that there's always room for improvement both in your marriage and in your business. Give each other credit where it's due, and encourage each other.

THE LESS YOU CONTROL, THE MORE YOU'LL ACCOMPLISH

We've mentioned the importance of letting go, delegating tasks appropriately, and letting our team members do their jobs in their own way. These strategies enable you to work smarter, not harder, because the less you control, the more you'll accomplish.

As you analyze your business and try to run it more efficiently and profitably, letting go of some things will give yourself more freedom. Remember , if your business is dependent on you, you only have a job. Your goal is to get your business to a point where it isn't dependent on you. Outsource what you can, or hire competent people. You can still focus on the high-level tasks that only you can do, but remember that there are highly talented specialists out there who can do an even better job at other tasks than you could.

Again, the more your business grows, the less you will be able to control every aspect of it. Being a great employee requires an entirely different skill set than being a great leader. When you have one job to do, you channel all your effort into excelling in that role. But when you are a leader—when you run a company—your main role is to achieve results through other people. You cannot control their level of effort or the manner in which they approach their jobs. That means you have to inspire and encourage them to do the best job possible—without having a hand in the actual work. Some people are never able to accomplish that.

Case in point: just because an athlete is superior in a sport doesn't mean he or she will make a great coach. Some team owners, general managers, and head coaches excel in leadership and also excelled in their respective sports. But that's not the case with all of them. Some athletes make great players but do not know how to achieve top results through other people. And that's OK. Those coaches who are excellent leaders, whether they played the sports or not, would never try to play every position on the team! In football, for example, there are eleven players on the field at a time, and it is rare that one player will play both offense and defense.

This is why coaches scout out players who excel in specific positions and then hire them, train and develop them, and continue to coach them.

We need to do this in our businesses as well. Provide the resources your team members need to do their jobs well. Communicate with them to find out what is going well for them and what isn't. Doing their jobs for them doesn't help anyone. Hire the best people, and then turn them loose! Focus on their outcomes, not on the way they carry out their responsibilities. Instead of micromanaging, leverage the skills and expertise of the people you hire.

The same principle applies if you are a solopreneur. Don't try to do everything yourself. Focus on your strengths and what you enjoy doing—those tasks only you can do—and use apps, software, and outsourced talent to accomplish the other tasks in the most efficient way.

The less you control, the more you will accomplish.

MAKE A LOT OF SMALL CHANGES TO CREATE BIG IMPACT

As the tagline for chapter 9 says, "Small changes can lead to big outcomes." Every business can use improvement. The areas that need help typically are not major business initiatives like sales or marketing. In our experience, most businesses need small changes in many different areas.

In our consulting business, I have had to make small changes, and they improved my efficiency considerably. For example, I realized I needed to spend less time on Zoom calls each week. I also had to spend less time volunteering. And finally, I began using automated tools to create more efficiency. Leveraging technology is a great way to improve your efficiency, whether you run a large company or a one-person shop.

There are a lot of little changes most entrepreneurs can make that will have a positive impact on their businesses. As we discussed earlier in our discussion about finances, some changes can lead to significant improvements. Those include increasing your prices, reducing costs, increasing the average sales per transaction, increasing work productivity, sending staff members to professional training, implementing new software, and updating equipment. Take a close look at your business and write down changes you can make. Document how they improved your efficiency and/or profitability.

The "devil's in the details," and so are the keys to growth. What are some small changes you can make in your business to make it more profitable and efficient? Ask your spouse to recommend changes, too, and make the changes you agree on. Then document the impact those changes made on your business.

GET HELP!

I have mentioned this several times, but it's so important that I'm mentioning it again! *Don't try to do everything in your business yourself.*

The first person you should seek help from is your spouse. Whether you work together or not, your spouses should be your chief counsel. I was discussing this with a friend one day, and he said, "Well, my wife doesn't work in the business, so I can't really rely on her to know some of the technical details."

I said, "That may be so, but she can still lend you the emotional, mental, and even spiritual support you need." Not to mention a fresh perspective. A lot of times, a spouse's intuition and overall views or feelings about people or situations can be valuable, even if they don't know the technical details of the business. Most spouses know enough about their significant others and their businesses that they can offer valuable advice, even without knowing the nuts and bolts of the business.

We recently completed an interview with Howard Behar for our podcast, "Power Up Your Marriage and Business™" (episode 96). Howard was the president of Starbucks International, North America, and chairman of the board over his twenty-year career with the company. He mentioned he would always take his wife on final interviews with job candidates. She didn't have to know the business or what position the candidate was interviewing for—she knew people.

Howard was in charge of the international expansion of Starbucks when it had only twenty-eight stores domestically. By the time he left the company, there were more than fifteen thousand locations. So he knew a thing or two about business, but he knew the foundation of every successful organization is its people. He trusted his wife's discernment when it came to hiring people of character and integrity.

Even before Kay Lee began working in the consulting business, I learned to rely on her intuition. One time, I was considering a real estate move. She did not have a good feeling about the deal or the business partner. Unwisely, I ignored her warning and moved ahead with it. It turned out that she was right! I would have saved money (lots of money!), time, agony, and effort if I had just listened to her!

Making a wrong business decision can be costly. If your spouse feels strongly about something, listen. Pay attention. Don't discount it. Remember, you are on the same team, working toward the same goals and vision. Respect his or her perspective and intuition.

In addition to seeking out help from your spouse, consider areas in which you and your business and marriage could benefit from guidance from professional. Seek out marriage counseling, business consulting, communication coaching, financial analysis, marketing strategy—whatever expertise you do not have. Remember, even the GOATs in professional sports have coaches! And even the coaches have coaches!

Again, don't wait until a crisis emerges to ask for help. Once you recognize that something isn't going well, get help. The longer you wait, the harder, more painful, and more costly it will be to fix a situation. Consultants and coaches aren't necessarily smarter than married entrepreneurs; we just see your situation from a fresh perspective.

A lot of times, we are too close to our own situations to see the big picture. As the old saying goes, we can't see the forest for the trees. we just see the obvious that you can't see the forest before the trees. When you're so ingrained in your business or your relationship, it's difficult to see obvious solutions that others can see. You are too emotionally attached and too deep into it to really see what's going on. Your coach, counselor, or consultant will serve as a valuable accountability for you as well. He or she will keep you moving forward and focused on what's important. We all need that kind of support! That is why I am in a mastermind group—accountability and fresh perspectives.

And finally, document everything! Write down your business plan, your vision statements for your business and marriage, and your strategy for the future. When it's written down, you can refer to it on a regular basis and change it as needed. Don't put it in a drawer and forget about it. Keep it visible. Refer to it during your weekly, monthly, quarterly, and annual meetings.

If you have not already done so, write down the high-level tasks only you can do in your business. Now write down which tasks you need to delegate to others.

We encourage you to stay focused as you strive for better balance between your work and marriage. Distractions will come at you from all directions! Remember what you're striving for, and keep moving. Small changes you make over time will lead to greater harmony. Following the strategies in this book, you and your spouse will learn to honor one another's individuality while working toward your shared goals, in tandem. This will make your collective efforts easier, more enjoyable, and more profitable, and it will enable you to create the balance you're seeking.

When you face difficulties, support one another. When you feel stuck, ask for help. And if something doesn't work the first time, try again. Before long, your small successes will evolve into significant progress.

> "Life is like riding a bicycle.
> To keep your balance, you must keep moving."
> ALBERT EINSTEIN

TANDEM BIKE CHECK

Scan the QR code shown below, or visit thetandembook.com/chapter-10, to watch a short video of us discussing this chapter. Also, you can download a free digital workbook that will help you create better balance in business and marriage.

A FINAL NOTE TO MARRIED ENTREPRENEURS

FROM ROBERT:

My heart goes out to all the hardworking entrepreneurs who are striving to be successful in business, often at the sacrifice of their home life, their marriage, and their family. It doesn't have to be that way, and that is the reason Kay Lee and I do what we do—we know from personal experience that there's a better way.

In our own families and in our own business, we have experienced many of the issues we've discussed in this book and have gone through a season of dealing with all of it ourselves. There have been times when I was working too hard (instead of smart) and neglecting Kay Lee and our marriage. That is not healthy for either spouse. No one wants to work all the time. Most people want more out of life than just working and succeeding in business.

Please don't believe the lie that in order to experience success in business, you have to sacrifice everything else. That's fake news! Don't accept that as normal. Ask yourself and your spouse, "How can we do this better?

How can we have a better life? How can we build a stronger business while also prioritizing each other and our family?"

And then do whatever it takes to live your best life together. Balancing marriage and business—and being successful at both—is possible.

FROM KAY LEE:

My heart goes out to the hardworking entrepreneurs whose businesses have become the "mistress." I am committed to helping married entrepreneurs who are struggling to provide a great living for their families while also keeping their marriages strong. You do not have to sacrifice one for the other; you can build a business, build a marriage, and succeed at both. That will look a little different for each couple or family, but the basic principles, which we have shared with you in this book, are the same.

We want you to increase your margin of time and money so you can live out your purpose. We want you to have a successful business while also having the freedom to really enjoy life with your spouse—both now and into the future.

Beginning on the next page is a checklist containing thirty-two strategies we have recommended in this book, along with space for you to add more strategies. There is room for you to write how you will implement or have implemented each strategy, on what date, and notes about the outcome and what you might follow up on in the future.

ACTION PLAN/CHECKLIST for Applying Our Strategies to Your Business

Action Item #	Strategy	How You Will Implement It	Date	Results/ Outcomes and Further Work Needed
1	Schedule an hour or two to discuss your marriage–work balance. What stereotypes about male and female roles might be affecting your relationship? When you have disagreements, what is the root cause? How do these issues affect your marriage and business? How do they affect your children, if applicable? Write a list of actions you will take to address these issues.			

Action Item #	Strategy	How You Will Implement It	Date	Results/ Outcomes and Further Work Needed
2	How do each of you react when there is a conflict? Do you avoid it, walk away and refuse to discuss it, blow it out of proportion, or raise your voice? Learning to resolve conflicts will benefit you in every area of life. What will you do to learn how to resolve conflict together? To get started, download our free "cheat sheet" that offers more strategies for resolving conflict in your marriage.			
3	Go back to chapter 5 in the book, and review the eight strategies for preventing conflict and the eight strategies for resolving conflict in your marriage. Which will you try first?			
4	When a disagreement arises, you can find common ground by asking each other clarifying questions. Commit to doing this in the future.			
5	Discuss your strengths and weaknesses. To what extent are you both handling tasks in the business that make use of your strengths? Take the DiSC Profile or another assessment. Then reassign or outsource any tasks you are doing that you are not good at and do not enjoy.			

Action Item #	Strategy	How You Will Implement It	Date	Results/ Outcomes and Further Work Needed
6	What percent of time do each of you spend working *in* the business (doing daily tasks to keep the business running)? What percentage do each of you spend working *on* the business (monitoring, planning, and setting your vision)? Strive for a 35/65 percent ratio. Download our free focus worksheet at https://www.thetandembook.com/chapter-8 to get started.			
7	Write down the tasks you both spend the most time on. Identify those tasks that are not the best use of your time, and delegate them or outsource them. Identify training your team members might need to take on these responsibilities, and provide it.			
8	How many hours do you both work each week, on average? How many would you prefer to work? What will you do to work less?			
9	In what areas do you need to ask for help–areas in which you do not excel but need to improve? What type of help or training do you need?			

Action Item #	Strategy	How You Will Implement It	Date	Results/ Outcomes and Further Work Needed
10	Aim for a profit margin above 10 percent. Profit margin is the ratio of profit remaining from sales after all expenses have been paid. To calculate your profit margin ratio, subtract total expenses from total revenue, and then divide this number by total expenses. The formula is Total Revenue - Total Expenses / Total Revenue. What is your profit margin now? What will you do to increase it?			
11	Analyze your pricing; enlist the help of a coach or consultant if needed. We have an eBook that describes four common pricing mistakes that entrepreneurs make. Price your products and/or services based on the value they represent to your customers.			
12	Charge a flat fee for providing a service that is pretty much the same for every customer; this will generate a higher margin than if you charge by the hour.			
13	What do each of you identify as your "love language," as described in Dr. Gary Chapman's book? The five love languages are words of affirmation, quality time, receiving gifts, acts of service, and physical touch. How will you begin supporting each other with your respective love languages in mind?			

Action Item #	Strategy	How You Will Implement It	Date	Results/ Outcomes and Further Work Needed
14’	Meet at least once per week for a business meeting, at the office. Mark these meetings as recurring events on both your calendars so you make them a priority. Share both positive and negative aspects your business regularly to increase your mutual trust and confidence.			
15	Do you sync your calendars? If not, consider doing so. How could this help you get on the same page?			
16	Be intentional about spending time together outside work. Schedule quality time together on your calendars regularly. Make specific plans, and honor them.			
17	Write down specific boundaries you and your spouse will establish to preserve your quality time.			
18	Brainstorm what you want to accomplish together. Share short- and long-term business and marriage goals. Them write a one-page vision for your marriage, and use it to guide the decisions you make. You can use our marriage vision template, available for free at TheTandemBook.com/chapter-4, to get started.			
19	Plan your vacation costs in advance, and save for them together.			

Action Item #	Strategy	How You Will Implement It	Date	Results/ Outcomes and Further Work Needed
20	Strive to make 80 percent of what you say to each other praise, and the other 20 percent should be gentle, respectful attention to areas that could use improvement or correction.			
21	To what extent are the two of you micromanagers? Discuss. If this is a tendency, commit to changing this behavior.			
22	Write a business plan if you don't already have one. Use our one-page business plan template, available for free at TheTandemBook.com/chapter-9.			
23	To determine your ideal amount of revenue, start by determining your ideal salary. Be sure to factor in inflation when planning.			
24	The most effective way to work smarter, not harder, is to position your business to scale. In general, *growth* occurs when a company adds new resources such as staff, capital, or technology, and its revenue increases as a result. In contrast, *scaling* occurs when revenue increases without a substantial increase in resources.			
25	Think like a franchisor. What types of systems and processes can you implement or automate that will allow your business to run more efficiently and without requiring your constant presence?			

Action Item #	Strategy	How You Will Implement It	Date	Results/ Outcomes and Further Work Needed
26	State your net-profit goal as a percentage rather than as a dollar amount.			
27	Net profit is what you have after all expenses, including the owner's salary, are paid. In the United States, the average net profit for a business was 7.7 percent at the beginning of 2021.			
28	Gross profit is the amount your company makes over a specific period of time, minus the cost of goods sold (e.g., raw materials, wages, taxes on your building). To increase gross profit margin, you need to raise prices, reduce costs, or both. To reduce costs without cutting expenses, sell more per transaction, and/or increase efficiency. Determine your ideal gross profit. How will you achieve it?			
29	Write down the key performance indicators (KPIs) for your business. Then commit to monitoring and improving them.			
30	If you employ team members in your business, consider tailoring rewards and incentives to each person's individual interests and passions. This will increase employee engagement, satisfaction, morale, and retention.			

Action Item #	Strategy	How You Will Implement It	Date	Results/ Outcomes and Further Work Needed
31	If you plan to launch an email marketing campaign, strive for a minimum "open rate" of 20 percent.			

PUTTING IT ALL TOGETHER

Our e-book, *Balance Business & Marriage Better*, summarizes key points we've made throughout this book. You can download it free

ABOUT THE AUTHORS and i61 Business Development

Robert and Kay Lee Fukui

i61 Business Development

115 W. California Blvd., #203

Pasadena, CA 91105

Phone:626.422.6628

Email: info@powercouplesbydesign.com

Website: marriedentrepreneur.co

Podcast: marriedentrepreneur.co/blog (on all major podcast players)

LinkedIn: linkedin.com/in/robertfukui

Facebook: acebook.com/powercouplesbydesign

Instagram: @PowerCouplesByDesign

Robert and Kay Lee Fukui are the cofounders of i61, inc., a business consulting company. They assist married entrepreneurs create better work/life balance by structuring the business to scale while giving precious time back to the owner to invest into his or her marriage.

Robert earned his marketing degree from San Jose State University and experienced twenty-five successful years in sales/marketing with companies such as Coca-Cola, Novartis Pharmaceutical, and Bristol-Myers Squibb. Playing instrumental roles in the launch of six major brands, Robert was directly responsible for more than $150 million in revenue, and he received national sales and leadership awards. His business acumen enables him to help family businesses build more profitable, efficient, and sustainable companies.

Kay Lee Fukui earned her business degree from the University of La Verne in La Verne, California. She worked in the banking industry for many years and in her family business as operations manager for more than 10 years before meeting the love of her life, Robert. She understands the highs and lows of running a family business and the sacrifices the owners make; often at the expense of marriage and family. Her passion is to see marriages flourish in the midst of building profitable businesses and to help entrepreneur couple understand that they don't have to sacrifice the marriage and family for the business.

Together, they have developed an innovative consulting program, Power Couples by Design™, which equips the married entrepreneur to build a thriving marriage *and* a prosperous business.

---

i61 is a business development network that exists to transform communities, cities, and nations by developing profitable businesses that positively impact people, culture, and economies (see Isaiah 61). Robert and Kay Lee Fukui solve entrepreneurs' business issues by creating the right profit margins that will allow their businesses to invest in the personnel, equipment, marketing, and other resources to drive their businesses forward. They believe profit + purpose = transformation.

TOPICS THEY SPEAK ON:

- Creating Better Balance in Marriage and Business
- Keys to Working Well as Husband and Wife
- Increasing Margin of Time and Money
- 8 Steps to a Thriving Marriage and Prosperous Business
- 4 Common Pricing Mistakes That Eat Profits
- Marketing Made Simple
- Faith, Family, and Finance: Keeping Priorities the Priority
- Succession Planning: Start Now
- Stop Being the Obstacle to Growth

SUGGESTED INTERVIEW QUESTIONS:

- As people get older, they tend to look back and wish they could have done some things differently. What are some of the top regrets successful entrepreneurs have?
- Being an entrepreneur can be challenging, and there are many demands from the business. There are also expectations from the spouse and family. How do you strike a proper work–life balance and meet these competing demands? Is this even possible?
- It seems as though the average business owner wears multiple hats, which leads to a heavy workload. That is what steals time away from their family. How do you fix that?
- Low profit is a common business issue that keeps many owners up at night. Is more sales always the answer?
- Your background is in marketing and sales, which is an area in which many businesses struggle. Why is this so hard for many? Is there a secret formula for marketing success?
- Working together as husband and wife can be a struggle. When would you recommend working together or not, and how can you prevent it from ruining a marriage?

Book Robert and Kay Lee as speakers for
your podcast, event, workshop, or seminar.
You can contact Robert at
RFukui@i61BusinessDevelopment.com
or 626.422.6628.

I61 OFFERS CUSTOMIZED SOLUTIONS IN THESE AND OTHER AREAS:

- Business-entity topics and contracts
- Business modeling
- Coaching
- Consulting in leadership and organizational change
- Marketing strategy
- Online courses
- Podcast
- Price and profit models
- Succession

Listen to our podcast

POWER UP YOUR MARRIAGE AND BUSINESS

Weekly episodes to help you and your spouse create greater work-life balance. You'll hear from us and some amazing guests that will help your marriage and business succeed.

On all major podcast players like Apple Podcast, Spotify, Stitcher and Amazon Music Podcast.

CHECK OUT OUR WEBSITE

for FREE and PAID resources to help you and your spouse create greater work–life balance.

POWER COUPLES

BY DESIGN™

From short webinars to self-paced courses to live coaching, there is something to help you and your spouse win in business and marriage.

50% off code on all paid self-paced courses:
TANDEM

SCAN QR TO GO TO WEBSITE

Follow us on Instagram and Facebook @PowerCouplesByDesign